Dark As Life 2.0

Edited by:
Tyree Campbell

Dark As Life 2.0
Edited by Tyree Campbell

All rights reserved. No part of this publication may be reproduced or transmitted in any form or by any means, electronic or mechanical, including photocopying or recording or by any information storage and retrieval systems, without expressed written consent of the author and/or artists.

All characters herein are fictitious, and any resemblance between them and actual people is strictly coincidental.

Story and poem copyrights owned by the respective authors
Cover art "Alone in the Forest" by Sandy DeLuca
Cover design by Laura Givens

First Printing, July 2024

Hiraeth Publishing
P.O. Box 1248
Tularosa, NM 88352

e-mail: hiraethsubs@yahoo.com

Visit www.hiraethsffh.com for science fiction, fantasy, horror, scifaiku, and more. While you are there, visit the Shop for books and more! **Support the small, independent press...**

Contents

Stories

10	Devotional by Tyree Campbell
30	The Girl in 114 by Trevor James Zaple
60	coming back home to a place I've never been by Laney Gaughan

Flash Fiction

49	Home Schooled by G. O. Clark
57	Siren With the Soft Sign by Nadia Gerassimenko

Poems

29	Slavery by Yuliia Vereta
48	An Acquired Taste by Debby Feo
54	Satan's Voice by Peter MacQuarrie
59	A Dead Wizard's Dust by Matthew Wilson

Features

51	Movie Review: King on Screen by Lee Clark Zumpe

parABnormal Magazine

H. David Blalock, ed
SUBSCRIPTIONS

parABnormal Magazine is a print digest [trade paperback format] released quarterly by Hiraeth Publishing, in March, June, September, and December. *ParABnormal* publishes original stories, articles, art, reviews, interviews, and poetry.

The subject matter of *parABnormal Magazine* is, yes, the paranormal. For us, this includes ghosts, spectres, haunts, various whisperers, and so forth. It also includes shapeshifters, mythological creatures, and creatures from various folklores. If your story also has science fiction or fantasy elements, we regard that as a plus.

1-year subscription:

https://www.hiraethsffh.com/product-page/parabnormal-magazine-subscription

Into Darkness Peering
Tyree Campbell [Ed.]

Stories inspired by a line from Poe's "The Raven"

Beware the Night Creatures by Bruce Boston
Damned Soles by V. F. Thompson
Resurrection Casserole by Sarina Dorie
The Sound of Burning Wood by Kendall Evans
Corn Maze by G. O. Clark
The Hand of Nephthys by Jennifer Crow
Too Much in the Sun by Mike Lee
A Death in the Family by G. O. Clark
Madame Astrofiammante's Curiosity Shop by
       Richard H. Durisen
Past Imperfect by Eric Lewis
Golden Dawn by Robert Beveridge
Immune by Terrie Leigh Relf
When Death Gives You Lemons by Tyree Campbell
Better Halves by KC Grifant
M by Russell Hemmell
The Takers by Rob Darnell

https://www.hiraethsffh.com/product-page/into-darkness-peering

It Came From Her Purse
Edited by Terrie Leigh Relf & Marcia Borell

We have enjoyed peering into all of these literal and figurative purses, not to mention a variety of containment systems! Viewing the contents of a woman's purse can be a frightening experience, or so I've been told . . . We would extend this fright to include men's satchels, go-bags, and such. Please join us in thanking all the artists, poets, and storywriters for reaching into their collective psyches to bring forth these oft quirky, occasionally demented, and definitely fantastical tales!

https://www.hiraethsffh.com/product-page/it-came-from-her-purse-edited-by-terrie-leigh-relf-marcia-borell

Devotional
Tyree Campbell

The last flake of old primer slipped from the window sill and onto the gritty pine floor to mingle with the others that had fallen over the years. Emily crossed her forearms along the rough bare wood and leaned through the opening. Moonlight the exact color of the little fish in the creek behind the house cast her freckled face in pure white and pious shadow and brightened her eyes to the blue of Rigel on a cold winter's night. Something dark moved in the clearing that separated the house from the forest--a nightbird, or perhaps a bat. It flitted down behind the irregular row of slabs of rotting wood and pitted granite that marked the cemetery, vectoring in on some insect fluttering among the family ghosts. Emily shivered. Something was always dying out there.

She knew the names on the markers by force of paternal rote. Pa had beaten them into her, branding her like a steer with the hot iron of vengeful memory. Her ancestors had moved here from eastern Kentucky just after the turn of the century. Ages varied, and causes of death. Smallpox, influenza, malnutrition. And gunshot, lots of gunshot. She counted the headstones to twenty seven, without seeing them. *These are your kin.* She always knew they were there. Sunlight glinted past them into her window in the morning, sharping her eyes. In the afternoon, the shadow of the house, a massive sundial gnomon, reached to the chipped granite stone over Orville Harper to tell her the time had come to prepare dinner with Ma. And at night the ghosts stirred to remind her of where she had come from and where she was going.

Emily had no need to look forward.

A wasp of wood stung her bare arm and broke off, and she pinched it free with her fingernails. The windowsill had started rotting two years ago, around the time the tornado scoured the ramshackle farms of Appalachian Tennessee, taking with it the chicken coop half a mile down the dirt road on Lee Mahon's patch of ground. Emily could repair the sill, given wood and tools. If they'd let her.

Noise from the living room caught her ear, and she turned around, eyes a little wider in the dark. Were they coming for her? A guffaw, a thump. Someone had stumbled. Vance, likely. At fifteen, a year her senior, he'd yet to take three gulps from a mason jar without losing his equilibrium. He frightened Emily. There were always little jabs and jests, but she sensed he meant his. That one night he would sneak into her bedroom.

Her brothers hated her for that bedroom. She was the only girl of seven children. She had to have her own room, especially now that she was "nubbin' up." It's only right, Pa'd said. But he'd looked at her when he said it like she'd leaked a glob of spittle from the side of her mouth.

Emily plucked the sweaty cotton fabric of the checkered dress from her chest and prayed for even the lightest of breezes to waft through the window. She was more than nubbing. She hoped she wouldn't have to suffer indignities. Polly Johnson'd had to wear a wool blanket to school under her thin hand-me-down dress, not able to afford unmentionables. And when the blanket had started to stain that day...

Emily glanced at the mattress on the floor. Something scurried past the folded blanket toward a dark corner to avoid her eyes--one of the field mice who'd taken up residence in the pile of logs outside the bedroom wall, she reckoned. She called them all Gus. There were fewer of them these days, now that the snakes had emerged from hibernation. Gus could have the blanket, unless she needed it for school. When the beans came in next month, she could hustle a few baskets down to the stalls just outside Murphysboro, perhaps sell enough to buy some more underthings from the Goodwill on Oak Street. Maybe she'd even find some aluminum cans or intact bottles alongside the road. If she could cash them in without Pa finding out about them, she might even have enough left over to buy a little bottle of metallic blue.

The living room fell conspiratorially quiet. Pa was not yet home from work down at Dale's Repair Shop, where he was waiting for a tractor part from UPS, and Ma was still quilting over at the Tanners. Emily shivered, and slipped to the mattress, lifting a corner to touch the security of the loose boards. During the past two years she had excavated a hidey-hole large enough to accommodate her and her dream. The silence frightened her. At any moment Vance or Jacob might stagger through her doorway, drooling and leering and steeped in sour mash. Practice had enabled her to conceal herself within ten seconds. But if she was not quick enough...if they learned of her excavation and of the secret it contained... No, she dared not risk that, not now.

Outside her door a board creaked, and she dropped the mattress and rose swiftly to her feet, stepping away just as Vance pushed the door open. In the shadows his face became a besotted caricature of itself, and his twisted smirk revealed the broken upper incisor.

"Get out of here," hissed Emily.

Vance slumped against the doorjamb, weight on his left leg. The belt of his jeans had come loose but not yet unbuckled. His shirt was open, two buttons missing. "Lessee um," he muttered. "I wanna see 'um."

"No."

Vance lurched toward the mattress and, stumbling, kicked it askew. As he stepped on one of the loose boards, it popped up. Emily held her breath. But Vance simply twisted his legs and flopped down onto the mattress, the impact jarring a rubber doll's head and a green pewter airplane next to the wall. He stretched out on his left side, crooked an elbow and brought his face to rest on his hand. Ready for the show.

"Lessee 'um," he commanded, momentarily sober. "Undo them buttons."

Refusal might lead to a physical conflict, and he would learn that he could force her compliance. Better to control the surrender, Emily reached back behind her and undid two buttons. It occurred to her that her deliberation merely heightened Vance's eagerness, and made him more determined. Feeling nauseous, she shrugged slightly, easing the dress top forward from her thin shoulders, but held the fabric strategically in place.

Abruptly Vance scrambled to his feet, and stood unsteadily. His finger shook as he pointed at her. "Take it off."

If she did, thought Emily, and let him see, he might leave. He might leave her alone this time. But he would come back, again and again, until... She keened an ear toward the doorway. "That's a door slam," she said quickly. "Pa's home. Get out of here now."

"I din't hear nuthin'."

"You know what Pa'll do he finds you here. He opens that front door, I scream."

Vance trudged toward the door like a dog who'd peed the floor and wanted to get away before the puddle was discovered. Emily waited until the door had closed, then rushed to the mattress, lifted the loose boards, and scuttled into her hidey-hole. As soon as Vance learned that Pa had not in fact returned home, he'd come back...and assume she had fled through the window. She crouched down in the darkness, drawing ragged breaths and fighting the raspy sounds they made. *If they heard, oh, God...* Her fingers located by touch the fragment of candle and the book of matches. Late at night when she worked on her dream, she dared light it, but not now, not now. In the dark, with Vance drunk and no one to protect her, she could only wait.

After a while she snaked a hand out and felt for her dream. Plastic that should have been cold felt warm, as if it had somehow come alive to her touch. Her fingers recognized the saucer, and read the tiny indented windows like Braille, and she took solace in the raw power of the engine pods. One day, if only.

Outcast at home by her gender, Emily was also outcast at school. Math and science were too easy for her--in elementary school she had been put forward two grades-- and still she shamed the boys with her swift and accurate responses, in class and on exams. Though she did not flaunt her scores, the girls eyed her with suspicion. What was she up to? Why was she interested in such things? Emily could have given them no clear answer. The daytime view from her window afforded her all she knew about life--that it began and ended violently or in sickness. But the view at night fed something within her that she was unable to define in words. And one day, in a store in Murphysboro, she chanced upon the symbol of that hunger. For three months, from November to February, she bought no lunch at school, hoarding her precious nickels and dimes. For three long months she added a ferocious plea to the compulsory nightly prayers: please don't let anyone else buy it. *Please let it be there.* Then, in early spring, while her parents and brothers were otherwise occupied, she ran three miles to the town and to the store and purchased a dream.

By this time the hidey-hole was large enough for her to fit into--not so much a shelter from abuse, though occasionally it did serve that purpose while Pa sobered or his anger waned, but as a refuge...a place to flee *to.* There, cowering in the dark, she might think and ponder and wish. The dream gave her meditations a form, a structure. This, she knew, was what was possible to her. One day, if only.

Above her she heard a scuffling. Vance or Jacob, perhaps both, had entered the bedroom in search of her. Though she had threatened Vance with exposure, in truth she dared not tell Pa about what he'd demanded of her. It was *her* fault she would have a woman's body, *her* fault that she tempted her brothers. Nor could she confide in Ma--whenever Pa administered punishment, Ma kept silent. She had no defender.

Her fingers closed around the plastic. Almost completed, it was. She needed only to cement a few more pieces together, then paint the finished starship the colors on the box. The starship *Voyager.* She'd heard of the show, and caught glimpses of episodes on some of the rare occasions when they visited someone who owned a television. Without the context of continuity, the episodes meant nothing to her. But the ship itself symbolized travel beyond dreams. Travel from here.

Escape from here.

Above her the scuffling stopped, and someone cursed in a low voice. Her door slammed shut. From somewhere far away she heard Pa's voice. She was safe for another day. She might emerge from the cocoon, and watch morning come to kill the stars.

* * *

The sun pierced the upper treeline to find Emily studying it through a smoked shard of glass. Mr. Hobbs was right, she thought, counting to three the sunspots. They might have been shadows of planets, so round they were. Mercury and Venus...she might go there one day, or to the moons of Jupiter. There were programs that might accept her. One day, if only. To Mars and Jupiter, and perhaps to infinity. But for now the smoky fragment was not large enough to shield both her eyes, and after a few minutes she had to pause and wipe away the tears that had formed, and with them the last crusts of sleep.

Behind her a board creaked, and she turned, but too late. Vance pinned her back against the window jamb and forced his hands under her blouse. A jagged fingernail caught at her flesh and tore it. In desperation she slashed at him with the smoked glass and opened a shallow gash in his left cheek, and blood welled.

Vance backed away and put a hand over the wound. "God*damn* you! You *cut* me, you little---"

"What's going on in here?" roared Pa, glaring at Emily. Under those terrible eyes she flinched, and dropped the incriminating shard.

"She *cut* me, Pa," cried Vance, pointing to it on the floor. "I din't do nuthin' and she *cut* me."

Pa unfastened his belt, and bent it double. "Turn around, girl."

"Pa, no," whimpered Emily, but she knew better than to hesitate or disobey. The leather strap whistled through the air and cut at her skin under the blouse, once, twice, and she bit her lip to keep from crying out. The third and last blow landed on a half-healed welt. A spark of pain exploded behind her eyes and buckled her knees, and she dropped to the floor, in too much agony to cry out. The welt was a souvenir of the striping she'd received four days earlier for, as the note from school said, "causing a ruckus." Dinosaurs *were* millions of years old, no matter what the textbooks said, but she resolved to keep her peace in class after that. Whippings were educational in that regard.

One day, if only.

"Bus be here in half an hour," Pa said, finessing the belt through the loops in his old jeans. His rough skin was dark with anger and last night's beard. "You hie yourself out there on time, girl."

Emily forced the words out. He had to hear them clearly, or he'd hit her again and again until he did. "Yes, Pa."

Left alone, Emily climbed back to her feet and trudged to the window. The smoked fragment had broken in two with the impact, and was now useless for her observations. Her eyes drifted downward, to the grave markers. There was plenty of room for more, in that field. One day they would all rest there--she, Ma and Pa, her brothers, and other kin. She wondered where they would place her marker...or whether they would give her a marker at all. Aunt Jackie once told her that her great grandmother and her aunt were buried out there, but no one knew where anymore. And there were low mounds, almost imperceptible and overgrown with grass, where girls were laid who had fallen to influenza or measles or a pox. They were spoken of in whispered memory...

One day, thought Emily, if only. Aunt Jackie had gotten out, moved to New Mexico after the Army and gone to college. If she could, Emily could...couldn't she? Like the fallen girls, Aunt Jackie was spoken of only in whispers, as if she had done something unspeakable . . . something to do with sex, Emily thought, though no one would ever say. To Emily she was a voice on the phone, tolerated only during the holidays. Emily had to let her dreams grow where she could hide them.

The door was closed, the front rooms quiet. She drifted to the hidey-hole and opened it, and lifted *Voyager* out into the light, where she might see it...where it belonged.

Her heart lifted as she set the trap door back in place and drew the mattress back over it. One day she might travel to the stars in such a craft. It was possible, she told herself, showing *Voyager* the sunlight through the window. *Do you see where you belong?* she asked the craft. It could happen. She could make it happen. For now, though, the plastic spaceship needed a coat of enamel, and she needed to gain an education without appearing to do so. She reckoned the enamel harder to come by.

"Schoolbus, Emily," Ma called, and with the memory of Pa's belt on her old bruise, she hid her dream back in the dark and then hied herself to the bus stop.

* * *

For Emily lunch was the highlight of the school day because she did not go to it, pocketing instead the three quarters and one dime the government gave her to buy food in the cafeteria. Her stomach muttered unpleasantly but bore up well enough as she sat on a bench on the perimeter of the schoolyard, where she might absorb the sunlight she so loved. In her lap a textbook fell open, an introductory to solid geometry for students two grades higher, and she absorbed that information as easily as her skin took to the sunlight. Other students passed by--boys, by the sound of their voices--and she ignored their caustic advice that a cookbook would prove of more use to her. Though she was accustomed to the jibes, they irritated her. She expected no approval from the ignorant, but surely there was someone in the school with whom she might talk about classwork.

An impact shook the bench--Amity Goodkind had just sat down beside her, dressed in a light floral print dress that fairly glistened in the sunlight and covered her chastely while allowing hints of the woman-to-be. Emily glanced at her once for identification, and withheld a greeting, for it was Amity whose protesting argument in science class had led to the note which had garnered Emily a striping. She held her finger on a figure in the geometry book and tried to focus, hoping that Amity would go away.

But Amity Goodkind was not that intuitive. "You were wrong the other day," she said, in a low, pleasant voice. "Those bones are Satan's tricks, to deceive us and lead us from the true years of the Good Book."

Emily said nothing.

"I feared you would mislead the other students," Amity went on, emboldened by Emily's silence and by a righteousness which wormed its way into her tone. "I feared your words would lead them to stray from the true path. I stood up for God. He created the Earth six thousand years ago. The years of those bones are false."

Emily's finger moved to another figure in silence.

"I wanted you to know that," said Amity.

Emily squeezed her eyes shut. *Don't say it. Don't . . .* "What makes you think I want to know that?" she asked, her lips tight and bloodless as she swore silently at herself for giving in.

The question seemed to startle Amity, and for long seconds she did not speak. Finally she whispered, "What did you say?"

"What makes you think---?"

Amity shot to her feet, and leaned slightly forward, pale eyes aflame as she faced Emily. Strands of yellow hair caught on her lips, but she ignored them. "Your *soul* is in mortal *danger* of the fires of eternal *damnation*, Emily Harper. I am *trying to save* you from that. Don't you *want*---?

"Go away."

Amity gasped. "*What?*"

At last Emily lifted her eyes from the geometric figures on the page. Amity Goodkind was actually perspiring with the effort of her imposed salvation. Her vacant gaze passed through Emily without effect. "Go. Away," Emily said again, and Amity's head jerked back as if Emily had poked a knife at it.

Amity took a step backwards, and another. Several students had paused to gawk, and she raised her voice clearly for their benefit. "Oh, I am gonna *tell*! I am *so* gonna tell..."

But Emily had already returned her attention to the book. Dimly she heard the slaps of Amity's shoes on the concrete sidewalk as she ran toward the school office, the sounds fading as the secants and cotangents reiterated their precise parables for Emily to solve. But presently her concentration flickered, and faded. Amity Goodkind *was* "gonna tell." In the hopes of forestalling another striping, Emily got up and headed for the Student Advisor's Office.

Emily felt eyes on her as she followed the sidewalk and the directional signs posted on the corner of the Admin Building. Already word had spread: she had rejected Amity Goodkind, she had rejected salvation. And dismissing Amity so peremptorily had not even been satisfying. She should have kept her peace and endured. As she passed the front office, she spied Amity remonstrating with Mr. Crocker, the Assistant Principal, but neither of them noticed her. At the door to the Student Advisor's Office Emily rapped sharply on the jamb and waited, hoping he was in and not out to lunch. The "Come in" afforded her a measure of relief.

Paul Archer sat at his desk with a "working lunch" of two bologna and cheese sandwiches and a can of Coke. The heat of the late spring day had rumpled his white shirt, and perspiration darkened his armpits. He finished swallowing and straightened his tie before he spoke. "Ah, Emily. I was just about to send for you from your history class. Please, sit down."

Emily did so, fresh spiders of worry scuttling up her spine. "To send for me, Mr. Archer?"

"It's about your proposed schedule for this fall, Emily," he said, sifting through stacks of papers on his desk. A graduate in Education Administration just three years before, he had accepted the position of Advisor at Redemption Public High School because no other positions were open, and he had become chronically overwhelmed by blank and half-completed forms. His face brightened when he found the one he sought. "Ah, yes, here we are." He placed the paper carefully on his desk blotter and read it once more, although Emily was fairly certain he had memorized it.

"Is there a problem with it, Mr. Archer?"

Archer sat back, and pushed the paper away. "Well," he began, and stopped. His pale brown eyebrows merged briefly, then parted. "Well," he said again, and closed his eyes as if in a silent search for words.

"I will take English Comp and History of Christianity in summer school," Emily pointed out. "With those required courses out of the way, I'll have room for another elective."

Archer cleared his throat. "Yes. Yes, of course. But...Chemistry?"

"Yes, sir."

"Emily...you haven't taken Home Economics yet."

Emily looked down at her feet. The sole at the toe of her left shoe was coming loose, and if she stepped into a puddle her sock would be sodden. "I'm not going to take Home Economics, Mr. Archer," she said quietly. "I'm going to take Chemistry."

"Emily, you can't graduate unless you take Home Economics."

"It's an elective course, Mr. Archer."

"Well, yes, it is, but---"

"Daniel Piersall and Isaac Sutton graduated, and they didn't take Home Economics."

Archer waved a dismissive hand. "Oh, but that's different. They're---" And he leaned forward slowly and folded his arms across the blotter and stared at Emily. "It doesn't sound to me as if you have a cooperative attitude toward your class scheduling, young lady," he said sternly. "It doesn't sound that way at all. It sounds to me as if some bad influences have begun to disrupt your thinking. Now, there are reasons for the district's school requirements, good reasons, and you cannot simply flaunt them just because you---"

"It's 'flout,' Mr. Archer."

"I beg your pardon?"

"The word you want is 'flout,' which means to show contempt for. I don't flaunt my attitude, Mr. Archer. I don't put on airs with it--at least, I hope I don't, and if I do, then I surely apologize for that. But I intend to go to college, Mr. Archer, and I don't think Home Economics will help me do that."

Archer reached for a stack of papers and began tamping it onto his blotter to straighten them into a neater stack. "Yes, well...we'll see, Miss Harper. Why don't you think about this over the weekend, and perhaps on Sunday you can pray to the Lord for guidance. You do attend services, don't you? You do pray?"

What does that have to do with Chemistry? thought Emily. Aloud, she said, "Yes, sir."

"Very well, then. I'll see you again on Monday, after you've had time to pray, and have thought this over. Ah, and that's the class bell."

Emily stood up. "I'll need a Tardy Note, Mr. Archer."

Archer found a blank sheet of paper, scribbled a note on it, and scrawled his name below, then passed it to Emily.

Only after she opened her textbook in history class did she recall her original reason for seeing Archer. But there was no help for it, not now, and she pushed her fears to the perimeter of her mind while she dealt with the day's lecture.

* * *

The scuttling spiders grew more active on Emily's spine as the bus approached her stop. Had the principal called? Did one of the boys bring a note home? But Ma was tending the stewpot and said Pa would be staying late at Dale's Repair Shop in Murphysboro, changing the spark plugs on Ben Farley's tractor and fighting with the timing. Emily hastened to her room and closed the door and stood still, leaning against it, heart racing, arms wrapped around her schoolbooks, pressing them to her breast as if they were the only things keeping her afloat.

It had been idiotic to respond to Amity Goodkind in any way, she saw that so clearly now. She might have withheld her question, might have kept her peace. Amity Goodkind was not relevant to her dreams. And to complicate matters further by challenging Mr. Archer on the relevance of Home Economics, well . . .

"Dumb, dumb, dumb," she muttered.

Of course, she hadn't actually said anything to Mr. Archer that would give Pa cause to stripe her, but a note home about it would surely upset him . . . and when the note about Amity Goodkind arrived on top of that . . . Emily shuddered. The welts on her back were beginning to itch, now that the healing had begun. She closed her eyes, and for a moment almost allowed herself to slump down the door to the floor. But that would mean surrender.

"No," she whispered savagely, and set the books on a small rickety table by her mattress. From an old military foot locker against a side wall next to the mattress she withdrew a worn and faded pair of blue jeans with one knee ripped open and the other almost worn through from kneeling while gardening, and put them on after removing her dress. Then she fished out a pale blue jersey and drew it on, and bound her hair with a rubber band, the chestnut pony tail dangling just to the nape of her neck. The entire outfit was her only defense. The fabric was thicker than that of the dress, and might better cushion the blows from Pa's belt, if it came to that. And although the jersey afforded her scant protection against the clumsy groping of Vance and Jacob, the jeans might thwart them long enough for her to find a way to escape.

Thus armored, Emily went into the kitchen, where Ma was still stirring the stew. "I'm going out to look for wild onions, Ma," she announced, and when Ma signified that she had heard, Emily walked out the front door, around to the back of the house, and quietly climbed into her bedroom through the unglassed window. Ten seconds later she was huddling in her hidey-hole, about to touch a candle to flame.

Illuminated, Emily felt secure: daylight in the bedroom above overwhelmed what little candlelight seeped through the cracks in the floorboards around the mattress. Only at night was firing a candle risky. Something light scrabbled over the left leg of her jeans, and she opened a cylindrical container and poured several seeds from it onto the dirt beside her leg. "Hello, Gus," she whispered, as the brown and gray mouse crept forward to investigate the snack.

After he had filled his cheek pouches and scurried off to tell his relatives of the trove, Emily turned her attention not to the model spacecraft resting on a sheet of cardboard on a ledge to her right, but to the underside of the floorboards above her. There ought to be stars there, she thought. She had no fluorescent paint, but she did have a bright red enamel nail polish she had never used, a Christmas gift from a distant aunt. Pa had called it "Jezebel paint" and had thrown it away, but Emily had retrieved it that night and secreted it in her hidey-hole. Yes, Jezebel paint for the stars. Amity Goodkind had spoken of eternal damnation--so be it. Hell for the stars was a fair trade, and she began to dab little red dots on the boards above, for Mars and Jupiter and the Red Spot, then for Betelgeuse and Arcturus and Antares, and all the other red stars she could think of.

Gus returned, and she set down more seeds for him. Grain from the skies, she supposed he thought. Gus did not question their origin or their purpose. The seeds were there--somehow--for him, and he made of them the best use that he could. *And the stars are for me. I don't know where they came from, or why they are there...but they are mine for the taking.* Her hand drifted out to the uncompleted starship, her touch the link between the dreams it represented and the dreams in her head. One day, if only. From a small box on the floor of the hidey-hole she withdrew a tube of cement with a sewing needle stuck through the end of it to keep the hole open. The clear viscous liquid within adhered to the needle as she drew it out, and carefully she touched it to each end of a strut and, following the guide, placed it carefully against the hull, holding it firmly there until the cement had dried.

"There, Gus," she said, when he or one of his relatives returned for more grain, "only seven more pieces and it's finished. What color should we paint it, do you think? Blue, like the example on the box? Or perhaps black, like space, with little twinkles like the stars all over the hull? What do you think, Gus?"

But Gus thought it was time to stuff his oral pouches and carry the loot back to his relatives.

"Maybe you have an Aunt Jackie," said Emily. "Maybe she knows what color it should be."

Aunt Jackie in New Mexico. She was far away...but not as far as the stars. If Emily could reach the stars, she could reach her. One day, if only. And in New Mexico she could bring *Voyager* into the sunlight and the starlight, where it belonged. Unexpectedly tempted by that vision, she nudged the floorboards upwards just a crack, just enough to see that the bedroom was unoccupied and the door was shut. Then, with a swift practiced move, she swept upward into the room, the hidey-hole door falling shut behind her and the mattress back into place, and she swept into the sky, into the stars, the starship in her right hand, arm extended as she danced, pirouetted, whirled around the room, her heart soaring just for a moment . . .

Only for a moment.

At the window she came to a halt, her eyes on the grave markers. Ashes to ashes, not stars to stars. And as if to remind her of that cold reality, the door to her room burst open. Emily whirled around, concealing the starship behind her. Pa had entered, brandishing a pair of notes. Behind him stood Jacob, smirking, for he had brought them home. Behind Jacob stood Ma, fretting.

"You just can't get yourself right, can you, girl?" snarled Pa, shaking the notes at her. His eyes smoldered like an open-hearth furnace. "That Goodkind girl says you rejected salvation, is that right?"

Emily lowered her eyes. "No, Pa."

Pa took a step closer, and yelled, "*Is that right?*"

"No, Pa, I didn't . . . I was just---"

"What's that you got behind you, girl?"

"Pa . . ."

"Let's see it, girl, and I mean *now*."

"Pa, don't---"

But he grabbed her roughly by the shoulder and spun her around, and the starship flew from her hands and broke in two on the floor, the saucer section skittering across the wood until it struck her mattress. At the door,

Jacob peered into the room, not daring to risk diverting Pa's wrath, but curious about the forbidden object, and behind him Ma fretted but made no move to defend her, and Emily saw all this as Pa spun her again and slammed her against the back wall of the bedroom, the impact jarring dust loose from the jambs of the unglassed window.

"It's the work of Satan!" roared Pa, and he stomped first one piece and then the other, and fragments of gray plastic flew in all directions while Emily's eyes went wide and she covered her mouth with both hands and tried not to cry out, though her eyes already were betraying her, and while she was staring in horror at the fragments Pa stripped off his belt and began to swing it with a fury Emily had never felt before.

"The work of Satan," and the leather strap tore at the back of her jersey and reopened the previous welts, and she refused to cry out, dropping to her hands and knees on the dirty wooden floor.

"I won't have it in my house," and the leather strap stung like lye like acid like a thousand hornets on the skin of her back, and Emily bit her lip to keep from crying out, and drops of blood as red as the stars she had dabbed in her hidey-hole began to splatter in the grit on the floor.

And then the blows fell in a deluge as Pa's yelling slipped to incoherence, spewing disjointed fragments about souls and Lords and Hells and sins. The blows rained on her arms, her shoulders, her back, her head, on old wounds and new ones, and she tried to scrabble away and to keep her penned he stepped too close to her and struck her with his fist instead of the belt, and the buckle cut into her back just above her right hip, and all the stars in the Universe exploded in the front of her skull, and she was in too much pain to cry out. She sprawled face down onto the floor, too weak to ward off the blows with her hands.

And the leather strap continued to tear at her jersey and her skin and her flesh, until her back was wet with blood and her ribs froze and she could not draw a breath, and her mouth left bloody smears in the grit on the floor.

And then it was over. Far away she felt footstomps, and heard a door slam. Her fingers clutched at the wood, tearing her nails, but she was in too much agony to feel any more pain. Her body began to tremble with the effort of revived respiration, and she made little sounds of, "Uhn-uh-uh, uhn-uh-uh," over and over and over.

Time telescoped, drawing out the pain. She might have lain there for an hour, a day, a year, as feeling returned to shriek at her, and she wanted nothing more than to lie still and die. She began to withdraw inside herself, away from the pain. If she could pull far enough inside, the pain could not reach her. But it pursued, as far inside as she fled. Wherever she went inside, the thunderhead of pain followed, waiting to burst open upon her when it caught her. And when she could withdraw no further, could only stand at the center of her life, it caught her, over and over again . . .

. . . and the room grew dim with the sinking of the sun, and shadows fell over her, turning the red to black. She was still alive. Her fingers twitched, and found a shard of plastic. She wanted to cry, and could not, she was in too much agony. She tried to breathe, and could not, her ribs ached and refused to obey her, but air whistled into her lungs and out, all the same. A splinter had lodged in her lip, but she lacked the strength to move her hand, to pinch it free. Gradually a numbness set in, dulling her mind though her body continued to shriek at her, and she bent a leg and pushed, and crooked an arm and pushed, and once more she was on her hands and knees on the floor, pony tail askew over her left shoulder and matted with blood from her back, rags of pale blue and dark red jersey hanging from her torso, and narrow crimson ribbons trickling down her bare arms.

Emily poised, gasping for breath. Her fingers closed around the plastic shard and a sharp edge of it bit into her palm, and she refused to cry out. Off to her left loomed the mattress. It promised a better cushion than the floor. Beside it lay pieces of the starship's saucer, and she began to weep softly. Tears mixed with blood on the floor below her face. With the deliberation of a sloth she moved a hand, a knee, dragging herself toward the mattress, collecting pieces of plastic along the way, ripping off her jersey to fashion from it a totebag, for there were far too many pieces of *Voyager* for her to carry them in her hands. She needed her hands for crawling. When finally the crown of her head butted the mattress, she felt surprised to have reached it. It was a simple matter, now, to pull herself on top of it and collapse. How she longed to do just that. If only.

But she was still alive.

Instead she fished a fresh jersey, this one lavender, from the foot locker and, gritting her teeth against the stinging of flesh torn again, drew it on. For a few moments she sat back on her haunches, rocking gently back and forth, trying to shut down her mind so that the pain could not get in. She wanted to think, and could not. But she could still see. She could envision what had to be done now.

And when she had brought the pain under control, she nudged the mattress aside, and opened the trap door to the hidey-hole and allowed herself to spill down into it. She landed in a heap on her shoulder and on her injured hip, and again bit her lip to keep from crying out. Her right hand clutched the totebag containing the fragments of her dream, and she drew it to her bosom to protect it while she squatted in the abyss. Her upper body rocked back and forth once more while she shut down her mind.

After Emily had gathered strength for one more vast effort, she stood up in the hidey-hole and tugged the mattress into position and let fall the hatch. Darkness enveloped her. And in that darkness she crouched, gasping for breath from the effort she had just made, the walls of the hidey-hole her support while she let her mind go numb and extend that numbness throughout her body. If she did not move now, she would be all right. She could breathe, and that was enough. The rest of her need only be numb, and she would be all right.

Later--and Emily did not know how much time had passed, though she was still crouching--boards creaked: someone had entered her room. Not Pa; the steps were too light, and uncertain. Ma, then. The light came on, and dim rays of it reached her in the hidey-hole. But the cracks in the floor were too narrow to allow her to see who had entered. More steps, toward the mattress, then to the back of the room and the window into the night. And someone else entered, heavier of foot. Pa? Emily heard words in a low and weak voice. Ma was speaking, and she keened her ears to hear. What was Ma saying?

But it was Pa's voice that she heard. ". . . git a flashlight and find her, drag her back here."

And then Ma said, "Let her be . . . she'll come back. She knows where she belongs."

Pa's growled reply was incoherent, but Emily heard more footsteps. And the door to her room slammed again.

Emily discovered that she had been holding her breath during the intrusion. Slowly she let it out, and held her body still while pain became a dull but terrible ache throughout her body. Thought required a deliberate effort, but she could think. Movement demanded the same effort, but she could move. If she could move, she could reach the stars and she could reach New Mexico and Aunt Jackie and be shunned and damned and whispered about with her, whatever it took, to reach the stars. If she could move . . .

Her hand could move to the candle, and she lit it. Her hands could move to the totebag, and she drew it open. Then to the tube with the sewing needle stopper.

And in the dim light of the candle she began to cement the fragments of the starship back together, one by one.

Slavery
Yuliia Vereta

A year after we were enslaved as a race,
The Comers realized we are ordinary.

Our home is no longer green like grass leaves,
Not alive like flamenco,
Not a bright flag among the free planets,
It is a new Gulag, a thickening of shadows.

Some are killed by the thirst to cover
The need for neurotic goods
With synthetic caress.

The world is no longer sound and fury, but a mad dance
Of blurred reality and empty eyes.

And it's only important to me
That late at night after zero
My puddles will rumble with ethyl.
So that I can forget this and remember
Shadows of extinct poplars,
Hoping no patrol sirens would be heard.

The Girl In 114
Trevor James Zaple

My mother told me her ghost story for the first time when I was four. I'd had the first nightmare that I can remember the night before. In that dream I'd walked through our living room with the light off, the familiar sofa and the floor cushions turned into barely seen hazards. As I walked through, trembling, ghosts jumped out at me. They were a vibrant, nearly-glowing purple, and shaped like the most stereotypical ghost you can imagine – a round shape topped with a bed sheet.

I had been inconsolable upon awakening, and it was only after ten twenty minutes of hugs and repeated gentle questioning that my mother managed to get me to talk about my dream. She listened carefully and told me that it was just a dream, and thereby nothing to worry about. She said that she had seen ghosts, and they didn't look anything like what I had described. They looked like we looked, only you could tell something was off. They blinked when you weren't looking, or they grew more insubstantial as the moon rose over the city.

I didn't understand most of what she told me then; it was the time during the formation of my first memories and I was still a neophyte to anything more than colors and shapes. It wasn't the last time I heard the story, though. From retellings throughout my life, I pieced together what I think is more or less the truth.

There was a murder. There is always a murder, to start. The sudden, vicious cutting of the soul from the body always creates a tear and allows certain energies to linger, or to come through from somewhere else. My mother was never sure which it was. After chasing my tail through the deep, dusty literature that attempts to categorize and analyze such things, it has come to my attention that it doesn't matter.

The kind of murder matters, though. In this case, it was one of the worst you can find: a father beating his child to death in the night. It was the sort of killing that you instinctively try to find a rationale for, knowing all the while that you'll never know exactly *why*. Maybe the father was one step from being fired and losing everything and the child woke him in the middle of the night. Or maybe she woke from a deep slumber to use the washroom only to find her father engaged with someone he should not have been engaged with, a prostitute or a drunk or perhaps even another child. The mind can spin up endless scenarios to fill in the unknown: witness the endless sequence of the names of God. In this case there never were satisfying answers. In the middle of a sweltering July night a man beat his child to death.

The father didn't go away for it, though. He used the usual nonsense such men spout when their sins catch up with them. He claimed she had fallen down the stairs of the apartment building earlier that day. When questioned sharply about why he hadn't taken her to the hospital, he would deliver an angry spiel about hospital wait times. Besides, he would claim, she had said she was fine. A few bruises, a headache. By the time she had taken a turn for the worse, it had been too late. His girlfriend, the girl's mother, had backed him up absolutely. The investigation dragged on – too few resources, too many crimes, the usual mantra – and before it could begin to bear fruit things began to happen.

My mother lived in the building at the time, a young woman building a love nest with my father in a ratty little one-bedroom in the sky overlooking the former glory of the neighborhood of Parkdale. When you worked odd jobs and temporary gigs, you had time to get to know the locals who did the same. The building was really two, a pair of once-formidable towers connected along the ground floor by a squat hallway that housed a jackleg convenience store they called a tuck shop. In the tuck shop the apartment dwellers would gather to rent pirated movies or buy loosies or simply to gossip. It was in one of these gossip sessions that my mother first heard of the girl's reappearance in and around 114, in the left tower.

It was just chance encounters at first, stoned kids wandering through the hallways between one place to chill or another. When you're in an altered state, it's much more comfortable to get off the elevator on the second floor and walk down to the exits. It avoids the problem where the elevator doors open in the lobby and there's a mixture of people ranging from disapproving elders from more traditionalist cultures to the overbearing and imposing Spanish woman who runs the rental office. Kids looking to avoid that scene, then, almost always pass through the hallway outside 114. One night, closer to the witching hour than not, a trio came out of the elevator and were halfway down the shabby hall when they saw the little girl standing in the middle of the dirty carpet. She didn't notice them, and they edged by her with wide eyes and disbelieving expressions on their faces. They could have lied to themselves later about the appearance just being some weird kid, but the side of the girl's head was stoved in and her eyes flickered. Even then, when her corporeal hold on reality was strongest, her eyes phased in and out of being. The old chestnut about the eyes being the window to the soul never supposed those windows being shattered with a brick.

Later, they would swear up and down that they wouldn't tell anyone, could never tell anyone. That night, two of them had sex on the couch of the third's apartment after that third nodded off watching the old Leo-MTV Romeo & Juliet. In the post-coital glow, one of the lovers managed to unstick themselves long enough to confess everything to their best friend, who lived in the right tower. From there, the chains of gossip carried it wherever speech carried on breath.

When my mother first heard it, she didn't believe it. Who would? The kids of West Lodge smoke strange things just to alleviate the stress and its adjacent feelings. They could have seen anything lurking in the hallway. After a while, though, she heard similar stories from different people, more dependable working people. They claimed to have seen the girl in the halls as well. Not just her hallway, but those above as well. Once in a while, in the early hours of the morning, you could sometimes see her in the lobby. She would stare at the strangely dated artwork and hover at the chains that gated off the fountains from the people who might have enjoyed them. My mother's neighbor, a Bosnian woman with tired brown eyes, once wondered why the girl didn't just go to the fountain. After all, she didn't even need to duck under the chain. Just, *whoosh*. The woman had a gesture my mother loved to imitate. A rise of the hand, a hesitation, and then a go-for-it follow-through, forward and then up, like an airplane taking off. *Whoosh*.

Once people got used to her appearing in hallways, she began to show up inside people's apartments. My mother always treated this unconsciously as a borderland for the story. In the days of the girl's haunting of the halls, she was bubbly, as though the whole situation were hilarious. As soon as she began appearing next to televisions and in bedrooms, she sobered up. Her voice grew quieter. She always seemed genuinely pained that anyone should have had to put up with anything quite so frightening.

Once, the girl appeared in my mother's own apartment. She lived on the tenth floor, so by that time the girl's range had grown quite far. My father was in bed. He usually had to get up at 6:30 in the morning to get across the city on the subway. My mother was still awake, watching late night television and sewing. When she got up and went to the kitchen to get a glass of water, she saw the girl sitting in the dining room, staring up at the ceiling. The skin around the sickly deep dent in her head had begun to pucker and the girl's hair had begun to grey just above her scalp. They looked at each other and my mother gave the girl her glass of water. The girl smiled and disappeared.

After that my mother was a regular wherever people gathered to speak idly. She lingered in the laundry room, by the elevators in the lobby, in the cluttered mystery of the tuck shop. She spoke about the weather, crime, news, and then would subtly steer the conversation toward the ghost of the girl. Not everyone saw her, but those who did were more than willing to divulge, once the plug was removed. She learned a dozen things, many of them conflicting. Many people just called her a ghost, and assumed she had the properties of ghosts from the cultures they descended from. Some said she was a vampire, and that her father had killed her to keep her from infecting the towers. Others thought her a witch. My mother said you could always tell who held that opinion. They would have salt lines in front of their doors, or they hung iron symbols, or wore amulets around their necks as they walked through the buildings.

One night there was a storm, a violent thing that blew up off Lake Ontario and whipped at the city. My mother watched the lightning arc across the city and then stood by the door, listening. The wind blew through the elevator shaft like whale cries, moaning and screaming in slow motion. Heavy footsteps passed by the door, and with them the sound of something being dragged along behind. Once, when I was back from college and we were deep into a second bottle of merlot, she said that she had felt a terrible urge to open the door. She didn't, though. She cowered by the door and waited for the footsteps and the dragging to disappear in the distance before she ran for her bedroom.

A few days later, a pair of police officers executing a welfare check on apartment 114 in the left tower of West Lodge found the girl's father propped up against the closet door of his bedroom. He was missing both of his arms. The evidence of their violent removal was splattered all around him, on the closet door, the cheap parquet flooring, the rarely painted baseboards. The girl's mother was not there. She was never seen again.

A pall fell over the towers afterwards. The gossip in the meeting places dried up. My mother fell pregnant with me one rainy night after going out for drinks. The autumn was wet and cold, and the jobs dried up in my father's industry. They made the decision to move out of the city. These were the days before you stopped finding places to live affordably even in the dead rural towns, and the tent cities swelled in numbers.

The city they moved to was haunted in its own right, by ghosts from broken homes, and it inspired my mother to scour the news and the message boards for word of the girl. A lot of the stuff was laughable. You had to filter through the cryptids, like the hairless and maggot-white Beast of Parkdale and the Tunnel Monster of Cabbagetown, and the head shop conspiracies like the alien base supposedly built under the city. Once in a while something with the ring of truth would turn up. When my mother came across someone mentioning a pale little girl, with greying hair and an awful wisdom that belied her seemingly tender years, she would print it out, cut around it so that it looked like a bubble, and paste it to a page of printer paper. She would then place it into a thick three-ring binder. I have that binder on my coffee table now, open to a page where the bubbles are in a ring around the open center of the page, where the only thing written, in heavy black permanent marker, is the word *WOW!*

Around that bold exclamation are posts from a thread specifically on the girl. They described sightings, encounters, speculation. The girl could be summoned, with the appropriate ritual, to deal with your cheating spouse. If you saw the girl at 3 AM in the hall you would suffer a loss the next day. The girl wanted to take your hand with her and carried a special curved knife to divest you of it. You could appease her by naming your most cherished friend, who would die within a week. The girl would appear to teenagers who snuck up onto the roof to smoke or drink or hook up, and they would have to stand on the ledge and close their eyes while she weighed them in judgement.

A few of them seemed closer to what might be truth. The girl appeared one night in the laundry room, staring forlornly at the window and ignoring the cries of the other people in there before vanishing between one second and the next. A maintenance worker, trying to figure out the source of a dripping noise that echoed through the 14th floor, opened the door into the stairwell and found the girl standing in the middle of the stairs, blood smeared around her mouth. Whose blood it was had never been ascertained. One of the local grifters, a spindly and softly melted-looking man who pretended to be a veteran to get better panhandling results, was seen speaking to the girl late one night as a snowstorm settled over the city. The grifter was found two nights later curled up in the entryway of the elementary school kitty-corner to the towers, frozen to the ground and to the thin, ratty blanket that was draped over him.

When I was seventeen my mother showed me these. Since then, I have memorized them. If the binder were to ever go missing, I would know these eyewitness statements forward and back. At the time, I begged her to put it aside.

Nights were difficult for me, then. I would come home from school to our little suburban hideaway and do homework while my father made his way home from work and my mother would read over her notes or spend some time writing and consolidating. She claimed to be writing a book, although I have never found solid chapters of any such work. I learned to fend for myself: to cook my own meals, to clean to an acceptable level of 'company ready', to keep the laundry cycle going. As I got older, my mother would disappear for days on end. She was always vague about where she went. It was a 'conference', or to meet a witness, or about a meeting with a bookseller or librarian to pick up some dusty collection of superstitions and folklore surrounding ghosts. Her leaving was never at set hours, either. On a few occasions she would wait until everyone was asleep and then slip out into the dark of the night.

When I came of age to drive, I decided to follow her on one of the more suspicious errands she left on. At the time I suspected her of cheating on my father. He took her oddity in stride, seeming to treat every vague assertion or half-formed itinerary with equal value. I was less equanimous about it. It is typical to be angry with your parents during the storms of adolescence and in this respect my mother made it easy. I quickly learned that raging at either of them would do nothing. My father would shrug and say that everyone has their hobbies, and my mother would merely ignore me. I turned it inward instead, seething in my bedroom and plotting out how I would expose my mother for what I thought were her obvious nocturnal activities.

She drove into the city, and I followed her, an hour on the 401 illuminated only by hard yellow artificial lights. When she pulled off onto the Jameson Avenue exit, I knew exactly where she was going. How could I not, after years of hearing her stories? Jameson, with its cramped and sweating Seventies-era apartment blocks looming over it like vultures. At the other end of it, those two horseshoe-shaped towers rising out of a jungle of crowded single-family homes. They were a revelation for me, something I'd heard about again and again but was then seeing for the first time. I parked a block down the street from where my mother had parked and made sure to keep back quite a way. I'd dressed in a black hoodie, but if she had turned to look, she probably would have recognized it. The night was dark, though, and the streetlights along the side street leading to the towers were only partially working.

She slipped through the back gate of the towers, and I followed in the shadows. There was only a darkened and dilapidated bit of playground equipment to greet us. Lights shone sporadically from the balconies above us. She entered the east tower through a door in the side of it, and I hesitated and lost.

I waited for her on the cold stone bench of a toppled stone table, near the fence that demarcated the property. West Lodge slept, the lights pockmarking its face only accentuating the darkness existing elsewhere. The night held still, but as I waited there for an eternity under cloud-threaded stars I began to feel as though I were not alone at the tumbled stone picnic setting. I refused to look, but I knew she was there. The girl my mother had undoubtedly come to find, sitting quietly beside me, her greying hair framing a face set with eyes that looked as though they'd seen centuries. Later, I would see that face in nightmares although I didn't look once at her that night. I couldn't. My own galloping fear paralyzed me into staring straight ahead into the unchanging face of West Lodge's east tower.

Some indeterminable time later I saw my mother coming back out through the same door she'd been through. I huddled myself into a crumpled little ball on the bench to look like another shadow among many, but she seemed deeply preoccupied and didn't even look in my direction. After she passed by me, I waited ten minutes before getting up and going to my own car.

I begged her to find another hobby, but I may as well have told her the daily variations in the price of hog futures. She was never one to choose my time or opinion over her obsession. Lately I'm not sure if obsession is the right word. An obsession implies a compulsion, something that must be done even if the reasons are unclear. An obsession necessitates a lack of choice. My mother's choices were clear-eyed and ruthless.

When she disappeared, it was difficult to feel anything besides a strange and guilt-inducing sense of satisfaction. It was the sort of feeling you get when you're building furniture and a piece that has refused to snap into its proper place finally locks in; there is a rush and a feeling that what was supposed to happen finally has. When I woke up on a dreary Wednesday morning to find the van gone and my mother with it, I had that sense. I didn't understand it until three days later when the Toronto police called to tell us that the missing van was parked behind a shoe store on Queen Street, only a few blocks from West Lodge. That call was the final push of the recalcitrant piece into its slot. The silence of the house after my father told me felt oddly right.

If her interests were not an obsession, perhaps mine were. I ignored my mother's piles of research for weeks, packing them up into boxes and putting them into the closet of her office. Then, bit by bit, I brought them back out. My curiosity got the better of me, and once I began reading through the information my mother gathered, I found it difficult to stop. Eventually I found my way onto the forums, where I discovered that the sightings and rumors had never stopped. I spent some time lurking and then dove in all at once. If I'd been in the dregs of my senior year then my journey to college might have been endangered, but my mother disappeared just shortly after the fireworks displays of early July. My father gently encouraged me to find gainful employment but as the days blended into each other I came to the subconscious decision that I already had.

The girl was greyer than ever, according to eyewitness accounts. A couple of the more recent posts indicated that her hair had begun to creep white. She had begun to appear during the day as well, at first in derelict parts of the towers but eventually in the halls, on the grounds, and once, remarkably, in the tuck shop. One poster, who seemed to have an inside track into the 11 Division police department, intimated that there were people looking to find the girl. I approached carefully, made casual talk in other sections of the forum, and cultivated a friendship with that poster.

It could have been completely made up out of a bent imagination, but there was enough of a ring of truth to it to make maintaining that relationship worthwhile. They could back up their posts with pictures, snapped surreptitiously and slightly shaky. Those images were just internal copies of police reports, at first; perfunctorily typed sheets detailing witness reports of the girl, appearing in lonely places to unsettled people. Then the reports shifted to the men who were trying to find the girl. There were complaints filed about them. They were local toughs but connected to people with influence. They knew guys in the blocks of south Parkdale, the warrens of brick mansions that had once been the toast of the town but had turned insular and mean since the money dried up. One image noted that there were people from all over the world, people who might pay good money for a ghost for one reason or another.

I took my obsession to college. My roommate was a pale English major who didn't ask many questions. I was able to pore over reports and sightings without her prying. When I disappeared on weekends, she never asked where I went or what I had done.

I went to West Lodge much as my mother had. From her notes, I knew the places I was most likely to encounter the girl. There were enough people living in the towers that there was always someone walking at the same time as me, so that I never looked out of place. The buildings were a mixture of recently arrived immigrants, students looking for a cheaper alternative to living close to the university, and the anarchist substrate that clung to Parkdale despite rising rents and gentrification. I fit in among them well, but I began to see men who did not. They wore herringbone suits but slouched, one hand held on their hips. Heads on swivels, they took in the entire view of wherever they walked with a casual, near-lazy approach. Whenever I saw them, I kept away, turning down random halls or taking the stairs.

    The men turned up more frequently in the posts about the girl. Other people noticed them, although no one wanted to dwell on them too much. A particularly brave forum veteran walked over to the towers one afternoon and cornered the property manager. Her usual gruff exterior melted away entirely, if the tale told held any accuracy. She refused to talk about the men or the girl, her skin curdled milk. When a man in a herringbone suit turned up in three pieces outside of the Skyline Diner up on Queen Street, it became apparent why. When there is blood being spilt, the best way to keep your own inside is to make your lips a thin, compact line.

    It fit the girl. The man's arms had been ripped from his torso and left haphazardly alongside his corpse. I studied the crime scene photos intently, my eyes lingering on the shreds of flesh that looked jagged and raw under the pitiless gaze of the police camera. Such force, such power, and yet underneath that efficiency, finesse. The negation of it. My grades slipped, and then plummeted. Lots of people suffer a culture shock in their first semester of college. I played it off as that to the advisors, promised to buckle down and get back on track.

    In late October the poster with the inside information from the police mentioned a raid that had happened near the towers, in a run-down house next to an art gallery someone had opened in an old convenience store. The police report mentioned a coven, and no one was sure if that was pig-headed masculinity cracking wise or if that was an accurate description. Alessandro DC, the police insider, said that the house was lived in by a 'bunch of Goths', which seemed to fit either possibility. He DM'd me later to mention that there were pictures he couldn't post even in the plausibly anonymous confines of the forum. By then I knew that he was really named Giuseppe and that his father had the unfortunate luck to have the case under his purview. Before that had been no big deal – merely having to compile crank reports from time to time, then bury them in filing. Now, a chill had settled over the department. Now it was real.

Giuseppe showed me the photos he couldn't post online. They were drawings, which surprised me. Many of the sketches were shaky, as though done in a panic by an artist of no real skill. Others were sharper, with heavier line weights and an air of flourish here and there. I recognized the girl, the towers, and my mother among the drawings. The 'Goths' were students of Renove, according to their statements, and they conjured his regard to reach out into the world around them and sketch powerful images that would hint at sources of great power. One of the women warned in her statement that sharing these pictures, allowing the eyes of others to fall on them, would cause deep and resounding waves of negative energy. Giuseppe's father dismissed the warnings, but Giuseppe wasn't ready to do the same. Holding the sketches in my hands, I was inclined to agree. They were heavier than they should by rights be, and they collected shadow on the page even as you angled them toward the light.

We parted ways amicably. He was young but passionate, invested in the story of the girl, and promised to tell me if there were any serious developments in the case his father was running. I felt bad about slipping one of the better sketches of my mother into my jacket, but only for a moment.

The seasons changed. The trees shook themselves bare and then slept under a blanket of wet white snow that froze in tortured shapes after Christmas. The girl appeared semi-regularly to scare drunks and teenagers, and once in a while she showed herself in the daylight, but even the most hardcore of ghost-watchers talked about how the girl's cycle seemed to be in a lull.

On the evening of Candlemas I was working late, trying in vain to find sources to support a paper I was writing on protest movements in the West versus those that became color revolutions in Georgia, Ukraine, and Kyrgyzstan. My roommate was sleeping, having come back from a lengthy night out. Out of a general sense of kindness, I was occupying a lonely table in a remote corner of the fifth floor of the library, my laptop blazing and my eyes drooping. Needing a break from my research, I flipped over to another tab where I had the ghost watcher forum open. There was a new post talking about a new apparition seen in the area, and it was a testament to my half-asleep state that it took my reading it three times before I realized that it was describing my mother.

She was described like the girl: there and not-there, at the same time, insubstantial but not transparent, a presence first felt and then seen. She appeared along with the girl, a grim guardian near a girl gone prematurely grey. This, alongside a news item about a pair of men in matching herringbone, dead in the parking lot of West Lodge with their throats ripped out. I closed my laptop in a hurry and left the library. The frigid temperatures made it so that no one saw me cross the campus under the ragged quarter moon.

Back at my dorm room, I recovered my keys and purse as quietly as I could. I was on the road ten minutes later, my headlights pointed unerringly toward that faded and slumbering neighborhood in south Toronto. On the way I called Giuseppe and received an earful about the sort of times that are appropriate to call, especially when it was about a subject that he was already informed on. He had, in fact, been ready to call me in the morning. According to his father, more strange men in suits had been seen wandering around the towers, stomping around enough that the normally police-shy residents had been making calls to 11 Division.

Approaching the city, it began to snow. As I turned onto Jameson it was hard to see the buildings. Lights loomed in and out of the swirling white wind and I felt as though the world had been reduced to the interior of my car. Crossing Queen Street was difficult, and pulling into the street that led to the towers taxed my driving to its limits. I had to park a long walk from West Lodge once my car couldn't make it any further. The storm covered my footprints as I walked past darkened houses.

I paused in the lobby of the west tower to warm my hands and shake the accumulated snow from my clothing. Next to the elevator, a man in a puffy black down-filled jacket stood watching the numbers above drop slowly toward the ground floor. He gave me a brief look and then returned to watching the car drop. When the car settled and the door opened, we both stepped inside. I studied the layout of buttons, wondering if I should start on the first floor or if I should go all the way to the top and work my way down. In the middle of this contemplation, I felt cold steel against the back of my neck.

"Just go about your business as you were going to," Puffy Jacket said in my ear. "Bring her out. Bring them both out."

I chose the top floor immediately. The gun barrel pressed into my flesh dug in impatiently as we drew closer.

"What are you hoping to accomplish here?" I asked him. I tried to keep my fear out of my voice but the condescension in his reply showed me I hadn't.

"Ghosts garner good money," he said. "Two ghosts will let me retire, if I sell them to the right person. And I have the right person."

"I'm sure," I replied, trying to put a brave face on the situation but knowing I had failed. We exited the elevator on the top floor, and I was driven forward into the hallway.

We walked up and down the hallways of the top floors of the west tower of West Lodge, keeping an even pace as dictated by my assailant. The doors were uniformly closed. If any of the people behind those doors heard us, they didn't open up to find out what was going on.

On the 14th floor I heard the howl of the wind in the elevator shaft, a series of overlapping moaning whale calls that burrowed into my head, shutting out everything else. I stopped outside of the stairwell. Puffy Jacket brandished his gun at me, but it didn't feel as threatening as it had before. He may have felt this as well, because he put it back in the jacket pocket with a haggard, confused expression.

"Why do you think I can lead you to them?" I asked. The whale calls echoing in the elevator shaft lingered between my question and his answer.

"We know who you are," he sneered. "We know who your mother is. You don't think she'll appear for you?"

"The girl never appeared for her parents, until the end of that," I replied. Puffy Jacket fell silent.

"If they don't appear for you," he said finally, "there'll be a third ghost to haunt this cursed place."

I stared at him, an idea coalescing in my head.

"What about the roof?" I asked. He grimaced.

"In this weather? Why would they appear on the roof, anyway?"

"Have you not done any research?" I asked, pouring all the scorn I felt for him into my voice. "The girl is said to appear before teenagers who go up to the roof for immoral purposes."

"We're hardly teenagers," he said disdainfully. I shrugged.

"Your purpose is immoral, though. Besides, do you have a better lead? Or is your idea to tramp up and down these halls all night until we both fall over?"

He had no reply to this. He took out his gun again and waved it in my face.

"The bullets in this are treated with a special solution given to me by the old woman who will pay me. She says they will bring ghosts who are already halfway into the world fully in, and then she can use their flesh."

I said nothing to this, although my stomach roiled.

"So if you think this is how you can draw either of them out," he continued, "then feel free and I shall follow. But if you think this is a ploy to get rid of me, you'll follow me over the side."

We took the elevator to the top floor in silence. I followed the signs to the roof, conscious of Puffy behind me with his special bullets. The door to the roof was heavy and putting all my weight into opening it drove me out into the teeth of the blizzard. My skin felt sliced open by a million tiny cuts, hard snow whipping against it in a fury. Behind me, I felt Puffy hesitate at leaving the warm interior of the apartment tower and I took the advantage. Slipping into the whirling snowstorm, I veered left into shadows, hoping to lose them. Behind me, stolen partially by the wind, I faintly heard him curse. This was followed by a gunshot and a sharp breeze to my right. He'd winged me with one of his precious bullets.

"I bet you can't hit me!" I screamed, turning my head to try to be heard above the storm. Silence followed this challenge. I lurked across the roof, with a vague plan to lead him around and get back to the entrance first, thereby locking him outside. I walked on a curve or turned without thinking in that all-encompassing white hell; my knees hit the low border wall and I pinwheeled my arms. I felt myself pitching forward, saw myself falling with an accelerating pace toward the blossoming ground, carried out into the parking lot by the force of the wind.

In one instant I fell forward; in the next, I felt arms wrap around me, pull me backwards. I fell over onto the snow, crunching it against the surface of the roof. It was paradoxically warm there, as though I had somehow ducked down under the wind and found a place where the warmth of hundreds of the lives below me radiated upwards.

Near my head I heard more snow crunching at cautious intervals. Feet, probably Puffy Jacket's. The wind fell into a lull, and I could hear his hoarse breathing. A presence rose next to me, and then Puffy Jacket cried out in surprise and pain. I rolled away from the sound and, as

I scrambled to my feet, the world exploded into the sound of a close gunshot.

My ears rang and even the tendrils of the storm wrapping fiercely around my head fell silent in the wake of the gunfire. Stumbling through the veil of snow I saw Puffy Jacket, his eyes wide and his hand clamped to the side of his neck. On the ground I saw my mother, a red flower blossoming from below her collarbone. I dropped to my knees beside her, ignoring Puffy Jacket altogether.

It had been long enough since I'd seen her that looking at her was like drinking ice cold water, delicious and thirst-inducing rather than quenching. I stared down at her and she smiled, really smiled at me for the first time in a long stretch of years. I smiled back – grinned, really – and my mind rushed my tongue into a tangle, trying to fit in everything I ever wanted to say to her.

"You have to protect her," she said, interrupting the flow of my thoughts. "There will be more coming for her, and you have to stop them."

I blinked, the tears half-freezing before being whipped away by the wind. All of my pleadings and loving words vanished. I stared at her as her smile fixed, and then her eyes glazed over into that peculiar pointed-at-nothing stare that demarcates the dead from the living. I looked away and saw fresh blood splattered against white snow, leading away out into the storm.

As I tracked him across the roof my mind was strangely blank. I knew that I should feel sad, perhaps wildly so, but there was no emotion in me. I tried to summon grief manually, bringing up memories from my childhood that my mother played a central role in, but stopped after a moment, feeling limp and empty.

In front of me, obscured by the storm, a pair of mismatched figures struggled. One was Puffy Jacket; the other was an apparition the size of a child, yanking on one of Puffy Jacket's arms. As I approached, the man's arm came free in a spray of warm crimson. He screamed mindlessly, the scream of an animal when the hunters close on it. The arm that the girl pulled away fell to the roof, blood flowing out of the ragged hole where it had once connected to a shoulder.

At the end of his other arm, a hand gripping a black pistol pointed up into the sky. Still screaming, he brought the gun down to be level with the girl. I stepped forward, wrestled with a hard gust of icy wind, and then slapped the pistol from his hand. It went spinning out into the snow and was lost. He stumbled toward me, stared haggardly into my face, and then lurched off toward the edge of the roof. He screamed once more, fading, as he fell.

I'm not sure how long it took me to come down off the roof. It was still night, but isn't it always? Things come in snatches to me, even now. Opening the roof door. The dirt encrusted in the hallway carpet, up close as I'd fallen to the floor in a wordless spasm of grief. The elevator, empty. The lobby, full of people speaking in loud grouped murmurs. The police maneuvering through the crowd, trying to disperse them firmly and failing.

Later, I sat out on the curb outside of the tower, staring at the clashing lights of emergency vehicles and trying to summon a coherent thought. At one point I closed my eyes, trying to will myself to be anywhere else. Eventually the police would find my mother's body on the roof and identify it. I knew inside my head that I needed to be gone, quickly, or the inevitable questions would grow more pointed. When I opened my eyes, a glass of water sat next to me on the curb.

I drank it, wondering at its crisp, fresh taste. *You have to protect her. There will be more coming for her.* My mother's words, the last things she ever spoke to me. I set the glass down on the curb. How could I? Was I to simply live here, in the hallways, become a ghost in all but death?

I set the empty glass to my side. My first stop would be Giuseppe. He would know, or he would know someone who would know. There was an old woman out there and my mother's death lay at her feet, her toes lapped by a pond of fresh blood. I got up and moved off into the snow, still falling fiercely among the streetlights. When I looked back, the glass had vanished.

An Acquired Taste
Debby Feo

At first the smell repelled him
But then soon it drew him in
Although he wasn't vampire
He desired to try some blood

Was just a "normal" human
He was not equipped with fangs
And he had no feeding needs
He just wondered of the taste

Started out with just his own
Just a few drops at a time
His wounds became much larger
And his energy was drawn

He started stealing blood bags
From the clinic where he worked
But that blood, it tasted old
As did blood from uncooked meat

He did an online search
Found a doable solution
Watering hole that welcomed
All bloodletting devotees

Home Schooled
G. O. Clark

She keeps the mist in a jar. Not any jar, but a bell jar from her father's Peruvian lab. Not any mist, but the mist from the surrounding jungle that glows at sunrise after the darkness of night retreats into the shadows.

More than one bell jar lines the shelves of her cloistered room, a couple acting as bookends, others lumped together like dusty teen sports trophies; her skills far from athletic, the only exercise she attempts is scientific field work.

The mist in each jar enshrouds the specimens within, shrunken to a more workable size by a process learned from her father the mad scientist, (her label, not his); the gold sign on his metal desk stating, Dr. A. Thorkel, PhD. On the wall behind, a half dozen framed diplomas of varying integrity.

She once had a snow globe, back in the states when young. A miniature Christmas tree, fake blizzard raging inside when shaken. Early on in her education, she shook one of the bell jars for a similar effect, but with tragic consequence. The little man within bashed against the opposite side of the glass, his bloody, broken remains turning the mist a pinkish red.

Live and learn, her father bemusedly told her, after consigning the smashed body to the furnace, and bell jar to the lab dishwasher for later use. Waste not, want not, he added over dinner, promising another father and daughter specimen hunt in the very near future.

Girls her age usually play with dolls; Tiny Tears, Raggedy Ann, American Girl, and Barbie. Dress them up, talk to them, place them at the head of their beds to keep them company, and silently bare witness. Static friends of cloth, wood and plastic; arms, legs and heads easily plucked off in fits of rage.

Her bed is void of everything but bedding now, her pajama-cozy self propped up with scientific journal in hand, reflected in her red framed reading glasses. Her mist filled bell jars and their barely alive tiny trapped occupants, encapsulated like bugs in amber, silent in the room's shadows.

She's been home schooled her whole life, along non-religious, scientific lines. Her mother died when she was only two years old, right around the same time her father began his experiments to save the environment, (literally shrink the human population to save Earth's resources). A tragic accident, he told her, leaving the dark details to her imagination. She keeps a framed photo of her on one of the bell jar shelves; a striking young woman of aquiline nose, green eyes and long red hair.

Her father's experiments continue, the Tinys (her term), who escaped his lab in years past somehow managing to survive deep in the jungle, procreating as if safe back home in their old cozy homes. Scientists and curious others who sought out the mysterious doctor, only to become the unwilling victims of his twisted experiments. They avoid the father/daughter duo at all costs now, attempts at killing the pair long ago abandoned, survival their main concern.

Her mind is filled with foggy memories. Half answers abound, but her inquisitive mind is kept too busy with their research to pursue them any further. She's sworn to secrecy, and doesn't really question his research methods. She learned how to dissect lab animals when preschool age. For now, she just cares for the specimens. He performs the more grisly tasks. All is copasetic.

Father and daughter are bound together by mutual love and their intense interest in solving the secrets of nature, and the template of creation. Exactly what is man, who is God, and who ultimately controls Earth's destiny.

Their findings will never be shared in the pages of *Nature, Science*, or any other vetted scientific journals.

For now, the mad Doctor and his daughter, experiment in secret, the outside world still in the dark, missing person reports filed away and forgotten. The doctor's twisted plan to save the environment, by literally shrinking the human footprint, jungle hidden; totally off the grid.

Movie Review: King on Screen
By Lee Clark Zumpe

'King on Screen' shows veneration, lacks objectivity, insight or cohesion

There's an American author familiar to horror fans, assuming they haven't been holed up in an attic or dwelled in a sewer system for the last 50 years in a life of voluntary seclusion, solitude and illiteracy. I first encountered his name around the time I started elementary school, and I watched as my parents added one dog-eared paperback after another to a shelf that would eventually be dominated by his work.

Of course, the author who piqued my parents' interest was Stephen King. The books that appeared on that shelf throughout the 1970s included "Carrie," "'Salem's Lot," "The Shining," "The Stand," "The Dead Zone" and "Night Shift."

In the early days, King shared that shelf with an eclectic assortment of writers, ranging from J.D. Salinger and Sherwood Anderson to John Steinbeck and Truman Capote. For those who think of King primarily as an author of horror fiction — he is widely regarded as the "King of Horror," after all — equating his genre output to the work some of America's most influential novelists might seem incongruous. But nothing about King's popularity, commercial success and prolific productivity invalidate the fact that he is both a major figure in American literature as well as a sheer force of nature.

Fact: King has written more than 60 novels. Fact: His books have sold more than 400 million copies. Fact: King has written at least 200 short stories, many of which appear in collections such as "Night Shift," "Skeleton Crew," "Nightmares & Dreamscapes" and "Everything's Eventual." Fact: At least 60 films have been produced based on King's work.

"King on Screen," a documentary film directed by Daphné Baiwir, examines how filmmakers have translated

King's fiction into cinematic form. The director sought out stories and unique points of view to show how King's comprehensive understanding of human psychology allows him to populate his stories with memorable, vibrant and complex characters.

Baiwir's film is a passionate tribute to King and to the many filmmakers who have adapted and interpreted his creations. Unfortunately, the director presents the material in a disorganized, unintelligible succession of interview excerpts and transitory clips from films and miniseries. The documentary never fully engages the viewer. Baiwir fails to impart her enthusiasm for King's work and for the dedication of so many filmmakers who have helmed King adaptations.

"King on Screen" opens with a crude fictional sequence in which Baiwir traverses a cheesy landscape permeated by visual references to King's universe. It's unnecessary filler that may appeal to diehard King fans, but the execution is so clumsy and inane that it simply serves as a convoluted distraction to most viewers. From there, Baiwir dives into an endless string of laudatory commentary from "an amazing cast of directors," as the film's Kickstarter page states.

In fact, so many directors contribute commentary that it's almost impossible to keep track of them without a reference guide. It's correspondingly difficult to discern at times which adaptations each of these directors oversaw, and how their interpretation of King's work was received both by audiences and the author himself.

Baiwir offers no unifying expository voice-over. She never posits a specific thesis or shares her own personal observations. She relies entirely on interviewees who deliver testimonials and anecdotes that never manage to coalesce into a cohesive narrative.

Instead of presenting unabridged commentary, the director has chosen to edit them into bite-size snippets and scatter them throughout the film. A few directors are allotted more substantial blocks of time, with Frank Darabont clearly the frontrunner in terms of visibility. Darabont is known for his adaptations of three of King's stories, including "The Shawshank Redemption" (1994), "The Green Mile" (1999) and "The Mist" (2007).

"King on Screen" avoids offering any critical analysis, either of individual films or of the entire body of work. There is no appraisal of poorly received films. There's no profile of the 1986 film "Maximum Overdrive," a film directed by King himself.

According to the entry on *Documentary*, penned by Annette Kuhn and Guy Westwell in "A Dictionary of Film Studies," a documentary is "a practice of filmmaking that deals with actual and factual (and usually contemporary) issues, institutions and people, whose purpose is to educate, inform, communicate, persuade, raise consciousness or satisfy curiosity."

Even if "King on Screen" is intended principally for diehard King fans, it is a disappointment. Any insights shared by interviewees are rendered lackluster and shallow by gawky editing and muddled delivery.

The lack of structure keeps the documentary from working even as simple listicle for anyone interested in prioritizing King cinematic treatments. Baiwir's obvious admiration of King overrides her objectivity and transforms this documentary into hagiography.

"King on Screen" opened in limited release in select theaters on Aug. 11. As of Sept. 8, the documentary has been available on demand through platforms such as Amazon Prime, Google Play and YouTube.

Lee Clark Zumpe is entertainment editor at Tampa Bay Newspapers, a Tomatometer-Approved Critic, and an author of short fiction appearing in select anthologies and magazines. Follow Lee at www.patreon.com/Haunter_of_the_Bijou.

Satan's Voice
Peter MacQuarrie

When I was a child –
   youthful and sweet
      and innocent and well-behaved,
  it came upon me and I
ignored it.

It followed
me to and fro – to the
playground and around and around –
I paid it no attention.

When I slept –
it came to me and asked
me many questions –
I paid it no attention.

It begun to promise me favors in
exchange for deeds done to others.
I paid no attention.

When I started college,
it appeared in lectures.
I wanted to know why,
so I asked it questions.

I asked
   it to stop,
     it persisted.

I paid it
   no more
     attention.

I found a soul mate and
   was a happy man as I could

       possibly be.

It promised me
   my woman would
      never leave or die.

So, I promised Satan's voice –
a promise
I regret to this very day.

Satan has my soul,
   and my soul mate
      now is gone to heaven
without me,
and I am lost to Hell.

My promise was to deny God,
And follow Satan to the lake of fire.

Some say I am
simply mad – insane,
and a broken person,
but I know the
truth about the
voice of Satan.

Siren With the Soft Sign
Nadia Gerassimenko

"A siren from the deep came to me
Sang my name, my longing
Still I write my songs about that dream of mine
Worth everything I may ever be"
— Nightwish, Ghost Love Score

You would not believe it. I could not believe it. Yet it did happen.

I met a woman once who did not age. That is a lie. She aged, ever so slowly—her words. One time she told me she felt trapped at age eighteen.

"My body has been corroding from the inside," she said. "It burns."

I could not tell; she looked like porcelain. Delicate yet calm and poised. As if she would not ever break, but could.

"No one believes me. It is unseen," she sighed. "My mind goes back to the before—my morning, my mourning. The burning has not reached me there yet."

She said it was a curse to be so young, to die so slow.

A witch cursed her in her dream. She told her to be beautiful she must burn to death. Ever. So. Slowly.

It was nonsense until it made sense.

The second time I met her, color returned to her cheeks. A faint smile formed at a corner of her rosy lips. Her eyes were to the floor; albeit, I could catch glimpses of hazel scintillating.

She explained she had another brush with the witch—in another dream. The witch took pity on her, took away some of the pain. But, not without condition.

"She told me to eat siren, with the soft sign," she almost murmured.

Siren with the soft sign was not a siren that wailed, or a siren that lured. No, it is how she called syringa—lilacs. And they became her syringe of sorts.

"I eat them in my dreams. The burning in me extinguishes. But soon so will I." She showed her arms in satin gloves.

One by one, she bared her hands shrouded in vines. My eyes widened.

"Less and lesser pain means a softer, faster demise."

Each time I saw her after, a flower bloomed on her and in her.

Her once fiery hair that cascaded to her hips were now climbing roses. Her hazel eyes could no longer see, dandelions poked out in their stead. Her lips, replaced with red tulips.

On an x-ray you could see giant pelican flowers for lungs. Her liver became watercress. Her veins grew to be leaves of dragon tree.

It was a miracle she could still breathe, could still utter words in monosyllables. I held on to what human was left of her.

The last time I saw her she was a flower bed, fragrant and sightly. Beguiling even, beckoning for me to fall and melt with her.

I could not believe in dreams becoming real. Yet it did happen. I was relieved I never dreamed.

I brought her a lilac—her favorite—or as she liked to call it: siren with the soft sign. I placed it to her bosom, her soft/ly bleeding heart now.

A Dead Wizard's Dust
Matthew Wilson

Creep softly for the shadow's teeth are long and sharp
But adventurers must be brave and they must be just
Now monsters guard the long dead wizard's dust
That villain who strung his king's intestines to a harp.

The painted demons on the wall dream with awful spite
And if you breath so quietly they will not wake
The dawn is not so far away if all you love is now at stake
Now mother's ill and the spellbook only works at night.

Children should not walk such castle ruins all alone
To find a cure for their sick mother far away
For shrieking bats shall wake the dead and here
      your soul will stay
Disturb not the wizard's dust who wished
      his best friend's throne.

coming back home to a place I've never been
Laney Gaughan

Brannoc was waiting at the luggage carousel by the time I got there. He knew what my bag looked like; I'd had the same one since high school, a beat-up duffle with the waxy ghosts of patches ironed and peeled off flaking the sides. He recognized the duffle before he recognized me, I had to wave to get his attention once he'd hefted it onto his shoulder, and there was a split-second blankness where I can tell he was trying to figure out where he knew me from.

I'm your sister, dumbass.

"Murphy, hi!" The crooked grin that immediately broke out was enough to ease my nerves. "You cut your hair, I didn't see you. I got your bag."

The haircut was an impulse decision, an appointment booked at 1:47 am in my apartment that I only went through with because my ex texted me she was canceling our joint Netflix subscription the morning of, and I was feeling pissy. It's a close taper up the sides, a swoop of gradient brown to honey across the top. According to my co-TA, it made me look "queer as fuck" which anyone who knew them knew was the highest compliment they could give.

It also, on reflection, looked very similar to the haircut my brother has sported since the seventh grade. It suited us both, I decided, swinging an arm over his shoulders in a half-hug. For a few, delicious years, I was the taller of the two of us, but that was ages ago. I've had to pop up my toes to hug him since the first time I visited for Christmas back in undergrad.

On the drive up to the house, I picked powdered chip fragments out of the various crannies at the front of the car, and hooked my phone up to the radio. Bran always drove - he's deaf in his left ear, so if he wanted to hear me, it was a given. It worked out; I liked to stare out the window. We had a year's worth of song recommendations to trade off, and I was halfway through picking a playlist photo from my camera roll – leaning towards the one from a hiking trip when we visited our uncle's cabin back when I was in middle school, with Brannoc getting the first of many bloody noses and baring teeth in a knit hat with bear's ears while it coagulated on his chin – when he hit me with the question I'd hoped to have at least a few hours more to prepare for.

"So, are we going to talk about Gigi?"

"Nope," I said, cropping my hand, gripping a too-short hiking stick out of the photo, and saving it as *Murph and Bran's Christmas 2018*. He accepted this with a nod. "Any way you can keep Mom and Dad from asking too much?"

"Will try, but also," he looks over at me, and we finish the thought simultaneously.

"It's Mom and Dad."

They liked Gigi a lot. Though they never said as much to me, I imagined they considered her a grounding influence. She was a financial advisor, a proper job, separate from the tangle of academia, where they feared I'd lose track of how the rest of the world lived. Gigi bought her clothes from the mall or online instead of fishing them out of huge trunks at flea markets, and went jogging on Saturday mornings. In spite of all of this, I'd liked her a lot, too.

Brannoc picked the next song, something old he must've heard on the radio at work, and I watched the concrete mausoleum of the airport pitter out into throngs of pine trees, dusted with frost like glittering jewels.

"I can't believe you stole my haircut," he said, as the music faded, and I scrolled through my recent listening for something appropriately folksy, sans banjos. Brannoc could stand a lot of my music, but he drew a firm line at banjos.

"You can't believe how much better I look in your haircut."

He and I always made the same expression in recognition of a dig, purse lipped smile with squinted eyes. I snorted and leaned back against the headrest, breathing in the music like cold air. It stirred and settled in my lungs.

He made a right turn around eight songs later, where the trees came to a staggering halt outside a Costco and corner mart. I blinked.

"Where are we?"

"They've been doing a shit ton of construction around here," Brannoc said. "Something to do with having to spend the money for tax reasons?"

I studied the unfamiliar buildings, somehow already suffering from chronic neon failure. A sign had been driven into the ground with a stake just off the edge of the road, the words a silt gray that must've once been white against red. *No Bones About It!* I could not place the slogan.

"Is that a liquor store?" We were only a few blocks from the high school, which to me seemed a cruel temptation. Brannoc nodded.

"I think they're just building stuff to build stuff."

Nonsensical legislative decisions, I supposed, were as much par for the course as anything in my hometown. I did miss the trees around this area, though. I'd used to take my camera on hikes to catch the light, broken into fractals by crisscrossing branches.

"Mom repainted your room," Brannoc said, as we pulled onto our street. "Be sure to notice."

"Roger that."

I adjusted my hair in the mirror and picked airline gristle from the corners of my eyes. Our house had always had a cherry-red painted door, but against the piles of unmelted snow clustered across the lawn, it looked particularly festive. Cold air stung my nose as I stepped out of the car, my boots scraping the salt peppering the drive.

"I missed you," Brannoc said, and having apparently exhausted his genuine affection quota for the trip, retreated to the trunk to get my bag.

"You too."

It was two days before I left the house again; two blessed, sleep-strewn days only intermittently interrupted by testing cookie batter with my Mom and helping Brannoc fill out a Tinder profile that said 'I like hunting and trucks but in a socially conscious, respecting women kind of way.' After this prolonged period of uselessness, I offered my services in retrieving a carton of milk, peppermint coffee creamer, and Canadian bacon from the grocery store.

New buildings had begun cropping up alongside the main road, their windows shuttered for the holidays and the signs on the doors difficult to read from this distance. There were a few political posters from the most recent election left to bleed ink on the turn into the parking lot. My scan as I waited for a chance to turn picked up another one of the gray and red ones, *No Bones About It!* I made a note to ask my folks about it when I got back.

A woman I recognized, but could not place, waved at me from the gallery of wilted flowers pressed up next to the cash register. I waved back, and hoped I was smiling enough that she wouldn't press too much further.

"*Murphy O'Hare*," she said brightly, just when I thought I'd made it into the clear. "I almost didn't recognize you. Look at your hair, it's so... modern."

I scruffed the fade up the sides with one hand, still enjoying the soft prickling.

"Thank you," I said, though I suspected it was not a compliment. The woman – who I thought might have been the mother of a grade school acquaintance – was eyeing me with the kind of puckered smile older people gave me when they were trying their damnedest not to look judgmental. Gigi always teased me that I dressed like a lesbian academic, which I couldn't argue with for several reasons, the least of which being that I *was* a lesbian academic. Like the jogging and online shopping, I suspected this was something she liked me in spite of, rather than for.

"Are you home for Christmas?"

I nodded. "I got back on Tuesday. There's been so much construction here, I could hardly find it."

If there was one thing that still passed for small talk in an age where talking about the weather was a recognized cliche, it was the universally deplorable burden of constant construction.

"Oh, I *know*," she shook her head, tsking. "It makes me so sad, so many beautiful forests. And for what? Another K-mart?"

On that, we were in stark agreement. I popped an additional bag of chips into my basket at the cash register, and tried hard not to recognize the cashier. I could have with focus, the younger sister of someone I'd gone to school with, possibly, but her eyes were wan from holiday shoppers, and she did not look in the mood to pretend she knew or cared who I was. I'd worked a few holiday breaks at the Joann Fabrics down the road during undergrad, and empathized.

I squeezed the air in the chip bag until it popped open in my car, and crunched while I waited for the windows to defog. On the opposite side of the road to the parking lot, a small patch of wood remained, and in it I saw a buck, its head sliding out from between the trees. Deer have this look about them, I always felt like they were looking at me. Maybe it's the abyssal darkness of their eyes, their ability to stand stone still. I've never been sure. Though rationally I knew I was in a car down the street with the windows blacked from an outside view, I felt as if we were making eye contact.

The buck shifted, suddenly, a kind of flinch running up its body, and then bolted forwards into the street. It took one step, and collapsed, crumpling to the asphalt.

"Shit." I brushed my chip dust off my lap and pulled out into the mostly deserted street, stalling on the shoulder where the road dipped into the woods. I wasn't a vet, but like every person with no knowledge of animal care, and a painful excess of empathy, I did not know how to leave things be. My boot crunched on the side of the road, as I knelt down by the deer.

It was still, pressed flat into the road, collapsed so thoroughly, I would've thought it had been run over had I not seen it fall myself. Tentative, and beneath my gloves, I reached out to touch its neck, feeling for a pulse. The skin sunk beneath my touch like an exhaling lung. I drew my hand back once, before reaching out again, towards the foot that had stumbled. The hoof was black, packed with dirt, and the leg was wiry thin. It, too, collapsed underneath my hand, a hollow space running up between the tendons and filaments where the bone should've been.

I swallowed, pressed the flat of my hand against the skull and then drew it back as if burned. The skin bent like fabric over air, sunken around the eyes and nose where a skull must've been moments ago but wasn't now, I was sure of it. Those dark eyes like marbles drooped out of their sockets.

I still felt as if they were looking at me.

"Woah, woah – slow down."

"I know I sound crazy."

Brannoc was clearing the steps that crept up to our front door, a process which involved as much beating the ice into shards with the point of the spade as it did actual shoveling. Our mother had likely grown weary of his sneaking finger-scoops of cookie dough from her ceramic mixing bowls.

He leaned down on the shovel, driving the point into the ice. "Murph - you always sound crazy."

He'd pulled down his hat far enough to plaster the swoop of hair to his forehead. Brannoc hated having his ears cold, had used to scream bloody murder when we went on hikes in the cold and clutch them with mittened hands like they were burning him. I'd told that story to my students once; it amused me to think that in their minds, forever, my brother would be a screaming four year old, cheeks ruddy from the cold.

I'd loved that screaming little kid, loved the moody pre-teen he'd grown into who would stalk around the upstairs playroom, and the pimply teenager who later would sneak beers out of our kitchen fridge and play the radio at full volume, but wouldn't go to the drive-in with his friends unless the move in question passed the Bechdel test because he had a big sister who helped raise him right.

I loved him most when he shrugged and dropped the shovel to leave a silhouette in the snow and said: "Let's go check it out, then," even though I knew it was partially because he wanted to get out of shoveling the sidewalk.

We curved up the road, with me watching the pines blur by, like I might be able to catch movement, even though we were the thing that was moving.

We reached the grocery store faster with Brannoc driving; the route he took was more of a loop, grazing up against the bit of forest rather than coming at it in a straight line. There was no deer on the side of the road when we got there, and something I think I must've known when as soon as I left. A boneless animal carcass was not the sort of thing left to rot on the side of a central avenue in a good, clean neighborhood like this one, with a brand new K-Mart and a new liquor store with five-sixths of the neon letters still intact. It was not the sort of thing to exist at all in a place like this, and how silly I must have been to have imagined I saw it there.

Brannoc didn't say that, of course.

Instead, he said: "City must've cleaned it up. Let's get drinks."

I nodded, numb against the window. *No Bones About It!* The sign across the street said.

"Who is that for?" I pointed.

"No clue. Those've been there forever."

"I don't remember them."

"You've been gone for a while."

It wasn't an accusation so much as an observation. I supposed it was a little on me; I'd left, changed and expected everything to stay the same in my stead. One of those double standards I tried not to hold – I could cut my hair, break my heart to pieces with the blunt end of a shovel, start telling people I was from the nearest recognizable city because explaining where my hometown was on a map got too tedious after a while, but home was supposed to be a photograph, something consistent to return to.

Brannoc had been fifteen when I left, and I realized now when he said we should get drinks, he meant at a pub, with an ID, and not me buying a six pack from the liquor store the next town over to drink in the car and toss to recycling before we got home. That he probably didn't crumple the cans as he drank them anymore because he'd realized that there was no point to it, that no one, least of all his sister, would be impressed.

Three drinks in, I decided the deer was a figment of my imagination.

Five drinks in, I started talking about Gigi.

"It wasn't *not* mutual." Brannoc sucked on a peanut shell from the little bowl in the center of the table and nodded. He'd slid in next to me in the stiff wooden booth, his deaf ear facing the chunky stained glass.. My hands tended to flap when I was drunk, the tendons unwinding like little plastic toys. I propped my head up on my knuckles. "But the worst thing is she's so damn practical about it. Like, here's *this month's rent, I'm staying with my sister.* I'm staring at a wall, and she's canceling our flights to Ontario and venmoing me the ticket. Ticket return - the money from the ticket."

I flung a wrist towards the bartender, and Brannoc carefully lowered my hand, shaking his head.

"Think you're good, Murph."

"And you know the most fucked up thing? I think I was in love with her," I shook my head. "I mean, *Jesus.* I always kinda thought we were gonna make it, even when things weren't great. Even when things were kinda awful, I was like, it's a rough patch, but this is my person, you know?" I stared at my brother's warped silhouette in the foamy glass, my chin resting on the table. "This my goddamn person."

The swirl of glass and orange bar lights that was Brannoc nodded once.

"You need to be careful around here, Murphy. This isn't the place you left."

He then bundled me up in his knit winter jacket and led me to the car, drove me back through the streets I didn't recognize to the house I thought I did. I'd forgotten the milk, the coffee creamer, the Canadian bacon, in the backseat; sitting like silent soldiers in tissue thin plastic. I almost reminded Brannoc about them, but drifted off before I could make the words solid.

The walls of my childhood bedroom were green, a brown-ish, mossy color that would not have looked out of place sprouting in lichen-y flakes along the side of an old stone wall. The quilt was technicolor, all earth tones next to the huge empty bookshelf, still bowing outward at the sides from when I squeezed my entire poetry collection into it when I was in college. I'd reasoned each volume was so small, it could hardly make a difference, hardly be the thing that could not fit.

I'd taken all the books to my apartment, but my parents hadn't moved the bookshelf. I stared at it until I saw eyes in the wood as the morning came to around me. I woke up like a cat, slowly testing the stretch and flex of all my limbs, feeling the joints pop, before I was satisfied enough to rise.

The outer pane of my bedroom window has frosted over, blurring the image beyond to a dull watercolor painting. I knew as soon as I walked downstairs, my parents would take a particular delight in the "good afternoon," as they had since I was a teenager first beginning to wake up past noon. When I reached the kitchen, though, the lights were off, the first floor vacant and soundless. I couldn't imagine being the first one up at this hour, but my imagination was thoroughly limited by the morning caffeine withdrawal and the dull throb of alcohol-induced dehydration in the back of my skull; I opted to begin my investigation by turning on the coffee maker.

Something heavy smacked against the glass screen door to the backyard. I flinched and turned, a small mass of black feathers lay crumpled on the deck.

My parents had never locked the back doors growing up and it seemed they still didn't; it slid open with a stutter as I pulled, cold air biting at my toes. I probably should've put on gloves, but I was in that half-awake daze where everything still feels like a dream. You don't pick up bacterial infections from dead animals in dreams. I knelt down, prodding the bird with my index finger. I didn't like the feel of it – squelching and soft, just tissue and liquid without anything holding it in place. I squeezed my eyes closed, and gripped the body with two hands, squeezing, feeling for something hard and brittle and bone-like. The bird made a wet, gurgling sound, and its orifices on either end oozed something dark and pungent.

I dropped it, closed my eyes and stumbled back into the kitchen, leaning over the sink to breath in the residue of lavender dish soap while my stomach writhed.

The bird had no bones.

The deer had no bones.

I scratched my fingers against the short sides of my hair and tried to breathe slowly.

"Murphy?"

I looked up. My mother, father, and brother stood at the front of the kitchen, frost dusting the shoulders of their jackets, their arms laden with shopping bags.

"Good afternoon," Mom said, grinning smugly, before looking over. "Sweetie, we can't leave the door open all the heat will get out." She paused when she saw the bird. "Oh, how sad. That's been happening more often. I think it's the construction – all the reflections get them confused. Can you take care of it, Bran?"

Brannoc was emptying the bags on the kitchen table: eggs, sour cream, apples, garlic powder. She was standing at the door to his left, so it was possible he hadn't heard, but the disassembly was more methodical than I'd come to expect from my brother.

"*Brannoc*," she repeated, louder. He looked up.

"Yeah, sure thing." Then, to me. "No, please, continue not helping."

Pursed lip, half-squint. I rolled my eyes.

"*Idiot*."

"*Weirdo.*"

"*Children,*" our father said. "Murph, wash your hands. Then *car*, and *groceries*."

My parents went to bed early; was much as it had used to frustrate me, most nights, I fought against the urge to mimic them. Gigi called me a homebody, more interested in period dramas on our – *her* – rose-patterned couch than club nights with her banking friends, who always went for hard liquor that tasted like gasoline.

I was going to miss that couch. It had been her grandmother's; we'd salvaged it from being sold the summer she moved into a nursing home. Getting it up the stairs to our apartment had been a pain in the ass, me breathing heavily, pretending my daily exercise routine was any more strenuous than walking with an open book in my hands. My arms had felt like noodles for days. Gigi had forbidden us from sitting on the fabric cushions in our sweating, dust covered states, so we'd ate pizza on the floor in front of the couch, soaking up the coolness of the hardwood like a pair of cats.

Sleep evaded me.

I slammed my knee into our family couch in the living room. Before I'd moved out, we'd had it a few inches back, pushed up to the wall. I sucked air through my teeth and rubbed the tender skin beneath my kneecap. It would bruise by the morning, and I'd press my index finger against it until it hurt over and over again, the same way I refreshed Gigi's instagram, refused to delete her number from my phone. If she called me, I'd recognize it. I'd answer, because things were not so black between us that she couldn't reach out if she needed help.

I filled the kettle from the tap and rummaged around the cabinets while I waited for it to boil. My mother's secret to a deep sleep: chamomile with honey and a dash of whiskey.

Moonlight glinted off the snow; I could see the yard clear to the edge of the forest. Something moved against the treeline: jerky, shambling, and bleached like bone. I told myself it was my reflection in the glass, and picked a mug from the cupboard above the dishwasher. The mug was salmon colored, *Don't talk to me before my coffee!* written in a blocky, headline font, gilded gold. I looked back out the window.

There was no movement. I was halfway through convincing myself there never had been when I saw the tracks; sections of snow kicked up and waded through just on the perimeter of the yard. Still holding the mug, I walked to the glass sliding door and wiped a strip of condensation clear with my pajama sleeve. Something had walked, or been dragged through the snow. Recently enough that I hadn't noticed before. Perhaps the thing I had told myself I didn't see.

My hand was on the latch to the sliding door when the kettle whistled.

I was in my pajamas – not the sexy silk ones I'd bought when Gigi and I got serious that clung with static to my skin every time except for when she linked her fingers beneath the elastic, setting my every nerve on fire, but the flannel bottoms with a fraying ribbon tie and a sweatshirt from my undergrad English department I'd worn down to softness over the years – and it was biting cold. I slept barefoot, and was barefoot now, toeing the dripped condensation from the door on the hardwood floors.

I could grab my boots and coat from the front closet, but the noise would wake everyone in the family save Brannoc, who slept with his hearing ear pressed into the pillow. I pictured my parents once again standing in the kitchen the same way they had when I'd tried to sneak out as a teenager. I would be as tongue tied now as I had then. In this house, I was still teenage Murphy, every stubbornness clouded with shame, every wound that much closer to the surface. I told Gigi on the drive out here, the one time she came to visit, that my parents would never see me as an adult, because I could never be an adult around them. She was an adult in their eyes, and when we were together, it seemed to rub off on me a little. This year I was their little, little girl, with a broken heart.

I returned to the kettle, and was generous pouring the whiskey.

I swallowed the tea in gulps before it had cooled enough not to scald.

I took a drive around town; there wasn't much to do except drive. As teenagers, we'd hung out at the local Target, walking laps around the aisles and talking about what we wanted to do when we left. The roads were different now; lanes had been appended to the narrow streets of my memory, fledgling neighborhoods popping up where once there'd only been trees. Stores I'd never seen before had already lost the luster of newness. I kept making turns to find out I wasn't where I expected to be.

I called Brannoc after the third time.

"Where the fuck is the Starbucks?"

He snorted. "Which one?"

"There's more than one now?"

"There's three," he said. "They're always packed, though, if you're looking for a quiet place to work. And don't you hate chain restaurants?"

"I am opposed to chain restaurants overwhelming small local businesses," I turned into a cul-de-sac and slowly looped past a row of identical houses. "Specifically ones that rely on unethical business practices and exploitation of labor. But I checked and we *have* no small local coffee shops, and I want a chocolate croissant."

"If you get me something I'll direct you there." I had planned on sending him a text to see if I could pick something up once I got there; I rolled my eyes. "Where are you now?"

"One of these weird Stepford neighborhoods. Next to where the Hobby Lobby used to be?"

"Hampton?"

"Sure." I pulled past another cul-de-sac and noticed a turn into a woodsy area. "Okay, I'm now going into the forest."

"That's a dead end."

"Perfect." The road was less clear in here, snow clustering the sides of the road, with over laden branches snapped in the surrounding trees. The path turned and kept turning, and suddenly I began to feel dizzy.

"Murph?"

"Was going to three point turn at the end, and now I feel like I'm going in circles."

"There isn't an end. Look, just turn around where you are." There was an edge to his voice, something concerned, almost panicked.

"What do you mean it doesn't end?"

The snow on the side of the road grew slushier, grayer, until suddenly it was hard, packed dirt flanking the sides. I blinked, slowed the car to a stop and looked outside. Through the woods, I could still see slices of neighborhood.

"What is this?"

"You should just turn around. You're not supposed to see that."

"See what–" My voice trailed off. On the interior side of the road, opposite the neighborhood, there was another side wedged into the dirt. *No Bones About it!,* much too far from any major street to make sense to have a sign.

"Murphy, just turn around. You don't live here anymore."

"One sec, and then I'll go."

He swore on the other end of the line. For years, I'd bit my tongue not cursing in front of him, only to drive him and a group of friends home from a baseball game one summer to hear them all swearing every other breath. So much effort wasted.

I switched the car into park, and slid out, my shoes cracking on the salt and sand on the road. I walked up to the sign and looked beyond it. A trail cut through the trees. I followed it, my breath misting in the air. At the end of the trail was a clearing, a hollow circle of trees with large white stones poking from the ground.

Only, they weren't stones. The skull of a deer the length of my arm sat half-submerged in the dirt, eye cavities filled with scuttling insects taking refuge in the shade. White bones protruded around the area like weeds, pointing upward, each taking a different shape. My eyes followed over to the trees themselves, which up close did not look to be made of wood at all. I stumbled backwards towards where I had come from. The panic came too slow, confusion preceding it and leaving me more lost and numb than scared. Metacarpals flexed where I'd thought the trees fringed into sticks. Wingbones, ribcages, femurs, skulls. Some the size I'd expect them to be, others surreally large.

Backing up, something snapped beneath my foot much too loudly to be a twig. I grit my teeth and did not look down. Instead I fled, scraping the key against the car door with trembling hands and lurching around around around until I found the neighborhood again. I had three missed calls from Brannoc, but when I got home and he met me at the door, neither of us said anything.

"I'm without a roommate at the moment."

My brother and I were curled on the couch opposite the television. Claymation figures that used to give me nightmares waltz across the screen, their features morphed and slumped and reassembled.

"You could move in with me if you wanted."

I tried to say it casually, like I hadn't been scheming all afternoon to gather him in blankets and haul my family across the city limits.

"With you?" We'd shared a bathroom growing up, seemingly perpetually knocking at each other's elbows. He'd started to sprawl once I'd left, leaving his razors out on the counter, still plugged into the wall. "Your school hiring?"

"I don't know." On screen, snow fell in papery clumps against the landscape. "Maybe. There's opportunities everywhere." Not for academics, of course. Not for a lot of things. My fellow TA's would've gaffawed at the statement. "You don't have to stay here, is what I mean."

Brannoc hadn't come to my room often in the middle of the night. I was always the one seeing monsters in the closets, in the dancing white lights behind closed lids. It'd shock me out of my half-asleep stupor when he knocked on the door. *Murphy,* this boy with pillow-fluffed hair the same color as mine. *Are you awake?*

"I know." *Bright festive music* played, according to the subtitles. "I like it here, though. It's home."

I was not always a good sister. The same way I wasn't always a good daughter, a good friend, a good student, a good teacher, a good roommate, a good partner. But I always hoped when Brannoc thought of me, he remembered sharing my twin bed with me and a mountain of stuffed animals. Of me wiping the condensation off the sill of his window and proclaiming the coast clear. Of me crawling under the bed in search of the phantom humming sound only he could hear.

"Besides I think Mom and Dad would go crazy if we both left. They'd get, like, a million cats." Clay humanoid shapes smiled unnaturally wide; their mouths could keep opening, just stretching and stretching until there was no body left, just thin lips looking into a cavern. They didn't. They closed again and kept singing.

"I know it seems weird to you," my brother said. "But I'm okay, Murph. Really."

My mother mastered the art of one-handed cooking when I was little. She could crack open eggs between her fingers, with the fingers of the other hand linked underneath the straps of my overalls to keep me from wandering to the stovetop to trace my fingers around the metal loops of the burners. The slots between them had felt like a maze I could only catch a faint glimpse of popped on my toes. My mother would knead bread dough with one hand, phone pressed to her ear with the other, listening to the audiologist office's hours while I built a block palisade around Brannoc in the living room.

The point being, she didn't *need* my help making meatballs. She never had. Not when I was seven laughing at the gooey way egg and breadcrumbs clung to her fingers, nor when I was sixteen, kneading the ground meat like it was my English teacher who'd docked points off my essay for being too political. There were times, cooking alone in my apartment where I would've snapped my finger bones along with the asparagus stalks to be completely and utterly superfluous in my mother's kitchen.

I scraped my spoon over the top of a cup of flour, and waited for the quiet to settle in the back of my mind. It didn't come. I watched my mother take off her wedding ring to go knuckle deep in the meatball mixture and found myself staring at the thin gold band sitting on the counter. Outside the window, our birdfeeder swung shallowly in the wind.

"It's so different here now. I barely recognize it."

"I know what you mean. Nothing is never really the same as you remember." Mom squeezed the mixture between her fingers and then bundled it back together into a lump on the countertop. "Look at *you*." She didn't touch my hair because her hands were goopy, but she looked at it. She used to sit on the couch and braid it with the comb wedged between her teeth. "In a good way, of course. I don't think things – or people – are meant to stay the same for too long. They get restless."

"I guess."

"And if people make us feel stagnant, it's okay to let them go."

It took me a moment to find the meaning.

"*Mom.*"

She held up her hands in surrender, ground chicken clinging to her fingers. "*I know, I know.* Bran said not to say anything."

I looked back at her wedding band on the counter. "I thought we were gonna make it. I was really sure. Now I'm not sure of anything. Of myself."

She was quiet for a moment, waiting for me to look up, perhaps. I didn't.

"You're yourself. You're Murphy. It's like this town. Faces, the outside changes. But it's the same bones underneath."

My parents had huge Adirondack chairs set out on the front porch, though we'd never been porch people. Our road was a flat stretch, rather than a cul-de-sac, so there was not much to see except for the forest on the opposing side. At night it was quiet, but never silent. Brannoc had left his boots out, and with my heavy socks, they slapped the floor like flippers. I swaddled into my comforter, and sat outside, my breath ghosting steam into the air.

The mind invents movement in the stillness, but I thought I saw something. There was the faint crunch of something breaking through the ice crusting over the snow. There was no need for a flashlight, this time of year. The snowfall collected moonlight until it shimmered. Something moved again, and did not stop, creeping out from between the trees.

The shape was a deer, and decidedly not a deer. It was partly a deer, with antlers spreading from its head like tree branches, fanning into white points. Its skull was attached to a spine with a ribcage that went on and on, bones sticking out from the spinal column like a centipede's legs. The ribs formed baubles; several unaffiliated ribcages had been strung together in place of a neck. Its front legs were too long, its back legs too short, and the bones themselves were attached to each other loosely, clumps of mud squeezed between joints, bits of torn fabric and hair tying them together in place.

Behind this shape was another, the second smaller, with several small skulls attached to its appendages. And then another, the third almost human in its build, with tiny skeletons like rats clawing around, trapped where its lungs should have been. The procession continued, mismatched bones threaded into new positions, stumbling their way down the street. I sat still, afraid to alert them by breathing. There were dozens, some with eye sockets in their skulls the length of my forearm, others with legs that went on and on, having to stoop to duck beneath the branches.

They walked down the street with a confidence I had lost in their sense of direction. The weaving roads, the haphazard buildings along the strip mall, everything that was no longer familiar to me I had the feeling was meant for them, these bone white creatures bleached in the moonlight, emerging and emerging and emerging from the forest.

I could no longer hold my breath, gasped louder than I should have.

The first creature stopped and turned. Black empty sockets with nothing behind them stared at me, abyssally dark. There was nothing beneath the bones that moved, no quivering heartbeat, stuttering breath. There was just the forest beyond. It studied me for a moment, and then turned forwards and continued down the road. I was a peculiar but harmless stranger in a lumpy comforter and too big boots, my short hair snapping with static and not protecting my ears from the cold. The others followed; I watched until my fingers went numb, and then turned and went inside.

Brannoc put on our playlist as we drove back to the airport, thumping his fingers against the steering wheel with the rhythm. Trees dwindled into garish concrete structures. My duffel bag sat in the back seat, stuffed to the seams, larger than it had been when I'd arrived.

"It was good to see you," I said, as we stalled outside the terminal, packed with rumbling cars and package-laden travellers.

"Yeah, sure."

I rolled my eyes. "Keep in touch, alright?"

He nodded.

A car behind us honked. My brother held up a middle finger the driver would have no way of seeing. I pulled my bag from the back and hugged it to my chest, resting my chin against the fabric. My apartment would be empty when I returned, and I expected that emptiness would crowd me out for a while. I would sleep better, though, in the bed I'd grown accustomed too over the past few years.

"You'll be okay?"

I looked over and tried not to see the twelve-year-old version of my brother.

"Yeah, I think so."

The air tasted of cigarette smoke and exhaust. I swung my duffel over my shoulder, and waved goodbye.

THERE'S A SALE GOING ON!!! IT'S STILL GOING ON!!!

BUY ALL THE BOOKS YOU WANT AND USE THIS 20% DISCOUNT CODE: BOOKS2024

THIS DISCOUNT CAN BE USED AS MANY TIMES AS YOU WISH, SO TAKE ADVANTAGE OF IT!

GO TO OUR SHOP AT WWW.HIRAETHSFFH.COM

NO MASKS, NO WAITING, AND WE NEVER CLOSE!